"This book is a comprehensive training workshop for effective leadership. It is intended for leaders that aspire to greater depths in their personal journey. Knowing oneself is the most certain way to achieve coherence when leading others with integrity. It offers a wide range of simple habits for life-long learning."

Álvaro Cedeño Molinari, *Expert in Peace and Conflict Transformation, Former Costa Rican Ambassador to Japan and the WTO*

"Bringing together global sources of wisdom with modern theories of leadership, *Seven Chakras of Leadership* offers readers a pathway for not only better performance, but greater well-being."

Dr. Lora Delgado, *Vanderbilt University, USA*

"Through a compelling fusion of leadership science and energy alignment, *Seven Chakras of Leadership* presents a groundbreaking framework for fostering balance, clarity, and purpose in the workplace. This essential guide empowers leaders to lead with authenticity while cultivating thriving, conscious organizations."

Angela Tafur, *Founder & CEO, eProfitable*

"Dr. Zohra Damani and Neal A. Bakshi take readers on an encouragingly reflective, yet empathetically gentle journey through the *Seven Chakras of Leadership*. The scholar–practitioner lens used by the authors makes it easy for readers to understand the relationship between balancing holistic energy and transformational workplace leadership."

Dr. Sherard A. Robbins, *Founder of Visceral Change*

"*Seven Chakras of Leadership* offers a groundbreaking blueprint for today's leaders by merging ancient wisdom with contemporary practices. This transformative guide empowers leaders to rebuild purpose, foster innovation, and reclaim balance—ultimately unlocking authentic, resilient leadership capable of creating organizations that thrive in challenging times. It is a must-read for any leader!"

Maria Assunta, *EY Winning Woman Entrepreneur & Founder of Honor Yoga*

"*Seven Chakras of Leadership* is a powerful framework for conscious leadership in today's complex world. Zohra Damani and Neal A. Bakshi masterfully blend ancient wisdom with modern leadership science, offering a transformative guide to balancing energy, emotional intelligence, and purpose. A must-read for any leader seeking to cultivate alignment, resilience, and authentic influence."

Travis Owen, *CEO, 1 True Health*

"*Seven Chakras of Leadership* blends ancient wisdom with contemporary leadership strategies, guiding readers to lead with purpose, balance, and authenticity. Damani and Bakshi provide essential tools for cultivating inner strength and clarity, making it a powerful resource for leaders seeking lasting transformation."

Vivek Upadhyay, *Physician and Biotechnology Executive*

"Most leadership books focus on strategy and tactics—*Seven Chakras of Leadership* goes deeper, addressing the energetic core of what makes a leader truly effective. By mapping leadership principles to the chakra system, this book offers a groundbreaking way to balance personal well-being with organizational success."

Bryan Wish, *CEO of Arcbound*

"Through a brilliant fusion of ancient wisdom and modern leadership principles, *Seven Chakras of Leadership* provides a transformative guide for conscious leaders. Zohra and Neal offer a powerful framework for inner alignment, creating a ripple effect that elevates teams and organizations. A must-read for those seeking purpose-driven leadership."

Ghita Tahiri, *Entrepreneur & Rapid Transformational Therapist*

"If you are looking for a new approach to solving the four most challenging concerns confronting both major corporations and individual companies, this is a must-read book. Companies are having to deal with widespread burnout, erosion of trust, stifled potential, and loss of purpose in both the employees and those in leadership positions. *Seven Chakras of Leadership* provides a new way of addressing these challenges. It is a well written and easy to understand model of leadership based upon the working experiences of both authors. I highly recommend this book. It provides solutions for the modern-day concerns confronting business."

Dr. Kenneth Harris, *Founder of Mind-Body Wellness Education Center*

Seven Chakras of Leadership

Seven Chakras of Leadership is a transformative guide for leaders seeking to align their inner energy with their professional impact. It connects ancient wisdom with modern leadership science, offering a powerful framework for navigating the complexities of today's workplace while staying grounded in authenticity and purpose.

At the book's core is the concept of The Journey—a practice inspired by Shamanism, inviting leaders to explore their inner world and align their energy centers, or chakras, to unlock their fullest leadership potential. The authors provide actionable tools rooted in ancient traditions—such as meditation, breathwork, energy healing, and chakra alignment—tailored to the demands of modern leadership. Using the chakra system as a framework, the book maps each chakra (root, sacral, solar plexus, heart, throat, third eye, and crown) to critical aspects of leadership development. By linking chakra principles to evidence-based practices such as emotional intelligence, mindfulness, and transformational leadership, leaders will gain practical insights into how balancing their energy centers can enhance decision-making, foster resilience, and improve team dynamics. Addressing both the empowering and shadow aspects of these energy centers, the book equips leaders with practical tools, reflective exercises, and action steps to navigate challenges, build self-awareness, and drive meaningful transformation in their organizations.

With templates for energy management and chakra assessment, whether you're a corporate executive, manager, or entrepreneur, this book equips you with practical strategies to balance your inner compass and develop conscious, compassionate leadership.

Zohra Damani is a visionary author, leadership strategist, and holistic practitioner dedicated to transforming personal and professional growth. With expertise in talent development, energy mastery, and transformational leadership, she empowers individuals and organizations to thrive.

Neal A. Bakshi is an author, speaker, business advisor, and spiritual guide who helps entrepreneurs and leaders reconnect with their souls to live an authentically fulfilling and peaceful life. By applying ancient wisdom to modern problems, he optimizes organizations, fosters genuine connection, and creates holistic perspective shifts.

Seven Chakras of Leadership

How to Create a Holistic Workplace

Zohra Damani and Neal A. Bakshi

Routledge
Taylor & Francis Group

NEW YORK AND LONDON

Designed cover image: @100 Covers

First published 2026
by Routledge
605 Third Avenue, New York, NY 10158

and by Routledge
4 Park Square, Milton Park, Abingdon, Oxon, OX14 4RN

*Routledge is an imprint of the Taylor & Francis Group,
an informa business*

© 2026 Zohra Damani and Neal A. Bakshi

The right of Zohra Damani and Neal A. Bakshi to be identified as authors of this work has been asserted in accordance with sections 77 and 78 of the Copyright, Designs and Patents Act 1988.

Trademark notice: Product or corporate names may be trademarks or registered trademarks and are used only for identification and explanation without intent to infringe.

ISBN: 978-1-041-06533-3 (hbk)
ISBN: 978-1-041-06298-1 (pbk)
ISBN: 978-1-003-63591-8 (ebk)

DOI: 10.4324/9781003635918

Typeset in Optima
by SPi Technologies India Pvt Ltd (Straive)

Contents

About the Authors

Zohra Damani is a visionary author, thought leader, and holistic practitioner who stands at the intersection of transformative thought, well-being, and talent development. She has authored two books, and this latest work marks her third, further solidifying her voice in the realms of leadership, personal transformation, and energetic awareness. As a trained Shamanic practitioner, Reiki Master, certified sound therapist, and spiritual life coach, Zohra is deeply attuned to the nuances of energy and personal evolution. Her passion for understanding human potential extends into technology, where she is developing an innovative platform designed to help individuals navigate and optimize their energetic states. With a career spanning People, Operations, and Strategy, across industries such as Consulting, Technology, EdTech, Law, Manufacturing, and Non-Profit organizations, Zohra has continuously shaped the ethos of workplace dynamics. Her ability to drive transformative change is rooted in her deep expertise in leadership development, talent strategy, and holistic approaches to professional growth.

Zohra holds a Doctorate of Education (Ed.D) in Learning and Leadership from Vanderbilt University, USA, reinforcing her commitment to driving meaningful change in organizations. Beyond her professional and academic pursuits, Zohra is a lifelong learner and dedicated practitioner of holistic wellness. Her certifications in yoga training and continued immersion in Shamanic studies—including advanced training in Scotland—reflect her deep commitment to integrating mind, body, and spirit in both personal and professional realms. Through her books, research, and innovative projects, Zohra continues to bridge the worlds of intellectual rigor, leadership, and energetic alignment, making a profound impact on individuals and organizations alike.

Neal A. Bakshi is the Founder of Awaken Mind Sciences. He is an author, TEDx speaker, angel medium, impact investor, spiritual guide, and global experience creator. His work emphasizes first-hand experiential healing, scientific and historical knowledge, and psychological analysis. He helps business leaders and individuals step into their new paradigm of life through complete perspective shifts. Neal's first book, *Banking on Angels*, was published in 2023. His teachings uniquely blend analytical thinking with spiritual intuition, making his work accessible to a wide audience of leaders and spiritual seekers.

Neal holds a Bachelor of Arts (B.A.) in Economics and History from New York University (NYU) and is a former Goldman Sachs investment banking vice president. He has meditated since the age of five and maintains certifications and training in over a dozen healing and wellness modalities, including life coaching, breathwork, bodywork, energy healing, sacred ceremonies, psychic mediumship, angelic channeling, remote viewing, astrology, numerology, pranayama meditation, creative visualization, and manifestation. Neal's passion is traveling around the world to connect healers, share indigenous wisdom, and activate the Earth's gridlines through spiritual ceremonies and experiences.

Foreword

There are some books that are meant to be read, but *Seven Chakras of Leadership: How to Create a Holistic Workspace* is meant to be experienced, adapting experimental elements and simple practices to our daily routine. Over the last 30 years, my personal transformation has consisted of many such adjustments to everyday life. It has been a healing journey discovering multiple levels of well-being and purpose. There are four core elements that emerge from this book that are central to my experience.

Peace

The first one is peace, understood as the ability to transform conflicts creatively, empathically, and harmoniously. Peace is a journey, not a destination, and this book resembles precisely a journey of peace. In that regard, what is most important is that we embody coherence, alignment, and integrity between our inner peace within ourselves, our inter-peace among human beings, and our outer peace with all other forms of life on planet Earth.

When referring to peace, it is pertinent to discuss the difference between conflict and crisis. A conflict is merely an incompatibility of goals. A crisis is a conflict system of several incompatibilities that are unknown, unplanned, and unforeseen. They are not mutually exclusive, but they require different tactical approaches. Both demand expert know-how and skillful facilitation. This is a rather unique form of leadership.

Consciousness

The second core element that resonates with me from this book is the experience of altered states of consciousness. Spoiler alert: psychedelics facilitate access to the source which can be accessed in multiple other ways. For example, the practice of achieving coherence between the seven Chakras that are described in this book produces a sensation that vibrates at a remarkably similar—if not the same—energetic frequency as a psychedelic journey. I mean it in terms of the perception of presence, authenticity, humility, gratitude, acceptance, and humility that come with this Chakra practice.

Completely unaware that I would be honored by the authors' request to write these words, I started practicing, seven months ago, at 4:30 am, the ritual of creating physical awareness and mindfulness of each one of my seven Chakras, moving from the root all the way up to the crown. What I didn't know then was everything this book has provided in terms of transversal connectivity, information, and resonance that each Chakra has with different aspects of who we are as human beings, which essentially means who we are as leaders.

A psychedelic journey or a transcendental meditation is an exploration of who we are in our most authentic version. This is achieved when we use our emotions as keys to open doors that lead to the source. There, we find presence, authenticity, gratitude, humility, acceptance, and forgiveness as mentioned above.

The resonance that results from exploring what the nervous system is capable of for each one of us, in every moment of our lives, is also very similar to the experience of exploring our seven Chakras. We go deep into our bodies with such focus and mindfulness that we engage within ourselves in a different realm of possibility. This leads me to believe that we may even go deeper with the Chakras to focus on dynamic elements of subatomic particles that compose every single molecule that vibrates in our bodies.

This book inspires the hypothetical question of whether we could heal ourselves by placing our minds and our focus at the quantum level of energy that we vibrate in. It would be fascinating if this could reveal the existence of a form of leadership that emerges from that quantum realm.

Another aspect of a psychedelic journey that resonates closely with the revelation of the energy of the seven Chakras is a Buddhist emotion that, for lack of a better translation, has been described as lovingkindness. This is a way of being from the heart, through love, and to do good to others and oneself.

The best way to enhance this emotion has been what I call hygienic journaling, or a way to cleanse what emerged during my restful hours of sleep that registered in my nervous system, in the memory of my dreams, in the most salient events of the day before, or the items on my agenda for the coming day by "writing it away." After 25 or 30 minutes of hygienic journaling, simply trying to name sensations from the body and emotions that emerge as the mind wakes up at the beginning of the day, the nervous system seems to fall into some form of calm restfulness.

This can be described as an unshakeable peace that stays with me throughout the day. This is a rather simple practice that has become a habit to engage emotions with curiosity, writing freely where they are, how they manifest, naming them, and figuring out ways in which they relate to other events in my past or future life. Engaging emotions with curiosity is a very effective way to open doors that lead to the source, quite similar to what emerges through the Chakra practice revealed in this book.

Then, there is the element of the Yin and Yang, the hot and the cold, the light and the dark, the far and the near, the inner and the outer, the loving and the fearful, the pleasant and the challenging, the fertile and the innocuous, and the animate and the inanimate. Everything that has one perspective will reveal its opposite. Although it feels that we live in such a dualistic world, at an energetic level, we are in the non-dualistic realm where there is no you and I, good or bad: there is just us. There just *is*.

Bioliteracy

The third core element that I briefly want to look at is the way in which the Chakras enrich our leadership to engage at a biospheric level with the ecosystem of all living organisms that co-inhabit planet Earth, including humanity. The idea of ecological bankruptcy might not be so significant to most people, but it might resonate with anyone whose nervous system is triggered by the word bankruptcy. In that sense, this is a friendly reminder about the ecological footprint that has exceeded the limits that plunder planet Earth, overcoming the planetary boundaries to sustain the levels of consumption that humanity has managed to develop since the Industrial Revolution.

In 1972, the United Nations got together for the first time to discuss a planetary crisis of an environmental nature. The science at the time revealed that pollution that was resulting from deforestation, internal combustion engines burning fossil fuels, and wasteful contamination of soils, aquifers, rivers, oceans, and forests was degrading the planet's ability to replenish the natural resources that we ordinarily extracted from it. Since that date, the world's population has tripled, and carbon dioxide emissions from industry pollution and deforestation have quadrupled. It means that in the last 53 years since we knew there was a global environmental problem, we've only managed to make it exponentially worse.

Impact means to leave the world better than we found it, and impact is what leaders do. Beyond having a net positive effect on the natural ecosystem is the notion of regeneration: enabling ecosystems to create wellbeing for the biosphere forever. We are fully capable of producing all the energy we need, all the food we consume, and all the water we demand in a way that we can regenerate natural ecosystems that have been degraded in the last 250 years. Becoming bioliterate means speaking the language of life, enhancing our agency to save ourselves while serving other life forms. That is the coherent leadership that is being called upon in this era, and this book awakens that possibility within us.

Family

Finally, the fourth core element that this book elicits is family. Reading it has been a constant reminder of the masculine and the feminine, which both manifest very strongly and clearly through me. It also reconnects me with my mother and my father, especially when, as a child, my mother's feminine energy was so nurturing, loving, and healing, while my father's masculine energy was so formative, stimulating, and encouraging.

Thirty years ago, I learned from my mother the art of physical relaxation, a mental review—in silence or with words, touching or visualizing the parts of the body—to become aware of every part of our integrity, from the toes all the way up to the head. This type of physical relaxation—as she called it and as I call it with my daughters since they were born—is described in this book as a fundamental practice to embody awareness. This is what effective leaders are all about: integrating and internalizing a coherent connection between body, mind, and emotions to lead oneself and to lead others. I regard this as an elemental principle of this book.

From my father, I learned a significant number of theoretical concepts and attributes of leadership. When I was graduating from sixth grade, he came to my classroom to speak about it. He gave a message that still resonates 38 years later: a good leader is one who shares their power. Throughout the following years of high school, college, university, and my early professional activity, and still today, as he is turning 86, my father has been a mentor and teacher of effective leadership facilitation within organizations, private and public, large and small. Learning from his practice through theory and bearing witness to some of his performances all those years ago, I have become fascinated with the topic of leadership.

Perhaps the most impactful practice that I have developed by observing him throughout most of my life has been journaling. His practice of reviewing ideas, emotions, and nervous system on scrap paper that he kept for as long as he needed before transcribing them is something that I adopted half of my life ago.

From my mother, I also learned the practice of meditation. She instructed me in the art of what she called turning your neon signs outside in, so that you could shed light internally and serve my internal needs before I could serve others. It was not a lesson that was learned easily. It took me decades to get to the point where I incorporated the principle of bringing light on my shadow before I could facilitate lighting others' shadows. This resonates highly with one of the key concepts of the book about acknowledging the shadow that every leader has.

The journey of reading *Seven Chakras of Leadership: How to Create a Holistic Workspace* has been formative at multiple levels. It has enriched my habits of well-being and purpose. It has reconnected me with my spiritual upbringing. It has revealed itself as a mirror to my deeper self, both the light and the shadow. May it be a flourishing journey for you too.

Álvaro Cedeño Molinari
Expert in Peace and Conflict Transformation
Former Costa Rican Ambassador to Japan and the WTO

Acknowledgments

First and foremost, I thank **God** for the opportunity to write this book, for the guidance, strength, and inspiration that have carried me through this journey.

To my **parents, Jafarali and Roshan Damani**, who may no longer be here in body but are always with me in spirit, guiding me in their own ways. Your love and wisdom continue to shape my path, and I feel your presence in every step I take.

To my **family, Jalal Damani, Nirmeen Rajani, Kalel, and Krish**, whose unwavering support and belief in me have been a constant source of encouragement. Your love is the foundation that allows me to pursue my passions and share my voice with the world.

A deep and heartfelt thank you to **Routledge** for believing in and supporting the unique concept we have brought to life in this book. Your trust in this work means everything, and I am grateful for the opportunity to share it with a wider audience.

To my **co-author, Neal A. Bakshi**, words cannot fully capture my gratitude. You have been more than just a co-author—you have been a force beyond this world. Your thoughts, your collaboration, and your words have inspired me in ways I never imagined. Writing this book with you has been an incredible journey, and I am profoundly grateful to have shared it with you.

To our **endorsers**, thank you for your support, your belief in this work, and for lending your voices to uplift this project. Your encouragement has been invaluable, and I deeply appreciate your contributions.

And lastly, to my **beautiful new additions to the family—Lucky and Chandra**. My dear feline companions, you have been by my side through every late-night writing session, keeping me company until 3 AM as I poured my heart into these pages. Your presence has brought me joy, comfort, and a reminder of the simple beauty in every moment.

With Love and Light,
Zohra Damani

Above all, I thank **God-Source** for utilizing me as a vessel to bring this book into being for the Highest Good of All. May this wisdom be the change our world needs to raise collective consciousness—from leadership, through organizations, to the products we consume, to all sentient beings on Earth.

To my mom, **Simi Bakshi**, whose light, blessings, and protection shine on me from the Other Side. Thank you for your unconditional love. You are the catalyst for my continual evolution on the physical plane and eternally in Spirit.

To my **family, teachers, friends, and mentors** across all my lived experiences—your support, wisdom, love, and guidance throughout the years have proven invaluable in this journey of life. No one goes through this journey alone, and for your presence, I am forever grateful.

To my co-author, **Zohra Damani**, you are so incredibly powerful. Thank you for being the strong, courageous, and perceptive channel to align the stars and bring this book into existence. You are Divine, you are Goddess.

A special thank you to **Routledge** and **Hannah Rich** for being the supportive publisher to bring this timeless leadership science to the world. We appreciate your ability to spread meaningful words for the continued growth and knowledge of individuals worldwide.

Lastly, thank you to our foreword author, **Álvaro Cedeño Molinari**, and our **endorsers**, for supporting this work to bring about a new leadership paradigm in the world. Your commitment to inner alignment and peace is the shining example for us all to look to.

With Gratitude,
Neal A. Bakshi

Introduction

The Case for Chakra Leadership

Understanding the Current Leadership Crisis

Corporate culture has lost its sheen.

From collective experience—spanning consulting, finance, nonprofits, manufacturing, and law firms—we've witnessed a pervasive challenge that transcends industries: the struggle of leaders to balance ego and soul. The higher they climb, the more pronounced this imbalance becomes, manifesting as burnout, misalignment with values, and cycles of disconnection that pass through teams and organizations. These challenges are professional and deeply personal, eroding morale, trust, and innovation in ways that stifle both individual and collective growth.

DOI: 10.4324/9781003635918-1

To call it a leadership challenge is an understatement. It is a crisis—one that is disintegrating the very foundations of organizations and communities alike and manifesting in the following ways:

- **Widespread Burnout:** Leaders are not just tired; they are depleted, operating from a place of survival rather than creativity or inspiration.
- **Erosion of Trust:** Misaligned leadership creates a ripple effect, fracturing trust between leaders and their teams, within organizations, and even across industries.
- **Stifled Potential:** Reactive, short-term decision-making traps leaders and organizations in cycles of mediocrity, squandering opportunities for growth and transformation.
- **Loss of Purpose:** Many leaders feel disconnected from the "why" of their work, their teams, and even themselves.

These issues take on even greater significance when considering the outsized influence of today's corporate institutions. The Fortune 500 measures the largest companies in the United States by revenue. Their impact on the world spans economic stability, social impact, and employee health to name a few. These companies employ over 30 million people worldwide and are collectively responsible for ~$19 trillion in revenue and over $40 trillion in market value.[1]

Zooming out, the Forbes Global 2000 companies account for nearly $52 trillion in revenue and roughly $240 trillion in assets across 61 nations.[2] The decisions at these institutions—made by a relatively small subset of C-suite executives, managers, and board members—ripple outward. From marketing campaigns to pricing strategies and employee wellness programs, these choices shape the mental and physical health of individuals within these corporate behemoths. The results influence consumer psychology, social equity, and financial welfare on a global scale.

A meaningful change for all begins with a change in corporate culture. A Gallup survey of over 15,000 employees in 2022 revealed that the ratio of engaged to actively disengaged employees had reached its lowest level in nearly a decade.[3] The greatest declines in engagement and employer satisfaction were observed among the youngest demographic of workers. Employees reported feeling increasingly uncared for, lacking encouragement for their development, and seeing fewer opportunities to learn and grow.

Furthermore, leaders today face a rapidly changing workforce dynamic, driven in part by the influence of Gen Z—a generation that prioritizes authenticity, social impact, and mental well-being in the workplace. Gen Z's expectations are a reflection of a larger cultural shift, one that values meaningful work, psychological safety, and alignment with core values. They seek leaders who embody purpose, not just performance, and organizations that stand for more than profit. Insights from Dr. Damani's recent research, conducted through hands-on collaboration with Gen Z in redefining training and onboarding strategies, further highlight this generational shift and its impact on leadership and workplace dynamics.

While this generational shift has brought important values to the forefront, this is not where the story begins. The early roots of corporate culture date back to the First Industrial Revolution, which lasted from 1760 to 1830. This time period saw increased mechanization and productivity with the likes of textile production, railways, and steamships. Yet, it was here that hierarchy with little consideration for employee well-being or organizational values began to take form.[4]

Just under a century later, we saw yet another exponential increase in technological advancements, science, and infrastructure with the Second Industrial Revolution. This time, however, social change became a hot-button topic with labor rights and social reforms brewing on the back of employees being treated like cogs on the assembly line rather than individuals. It wasn't until the early 20th century that the human relations movement began to flourish with the Hawthorne Experiments. These surveys, conducted in an Illinois factory, showed that social factors were as important as financial incentives in improving employee productivity.[5]

Fast-forward to the present, and in the wake of the COVID-19 pandemic, millions of workers have reevaluated their priorities around personal balance and career fulfillment. This shift gave rise to phenomena like the Great Resignation and Quiet Quitting.[3] The onus of this corporate exodus falls on the leaders of these organizations, highlighting a growing demand for compassionate and empathetic leaders who embody strength and empowerment through self-awareness and intentional, purposeful work.[6]

As we foray into exponential increase in technology, communication, and financial decentralization, we stand at an important inflection point. This moment calls for a bold reimagining of leadership for the "new earth" we are shaping. It is an invitation to weave together the lessons of history with the demands of the present and the boundless possibilities of the future. By doing so, we give rise to a leadership model that harmonizes inner coherence with external effectiveness.

But this begs the question: how can leaders reconnect with their own purpose and values, create environments that inspire, and navigate the growing complexity of modern challenges with clarity and balance? How can they move beyond the transactional, ego-driven models of the past to lead with authenticity, passion, and alignment?

The answers to these questions begin with the leaders themselves. Only by engaging in the inner work—through reconnecting with their core values, cultivating balance, and aligning their energy—can leaders build the thriving, purpose-driven cultures that today's workforce and organizations demand. Concepts such as alignment, flow, and balance—once described in spiritual terms as "energy" or "vibes"—are now finding resonance in modern science and psychology. This reminds us that leadership is not merely a transactional process but a deeply human one, rooted in the connection between mind, body, and spirit.

The current society is increasingly defined by speed, complexity, and change; hence, these principles offer leaders a grounded framework for navigating uncertainty as they keep orienting their inner compass. Balance is not a static state but a dynamic process of recalibration, and that true leadership begins within—by cultivating clarity, presence, and purpose.

This is where Chakra Leadership (CL) comes in. We developed this holistic framework to align a leader's inner world with their external impact by offering a roadmap for addressing burnout, misalignment, and disconnection while fostering a sense of balance, purpose, and authentic relating. Through this approach, leaders can move beyond simply managing their teams to empowering and inspiring them.

But what does that even look like for leaders, and how does this show up in organizations?

Bridging Leadership and Chakras

The authors collectively share decades of experience inside some of the largest corporations in the world—from a vice president closing $100 billion of deals at Goldman Sachs to organizational leadership expertise at Meta, Starbucks, and EY. These corporate experiences intertwine with their personal journeys, which have led them to integrate holistic wellness practices through the understanding of the subtle energy centers in the body, known as chakras. First introduced in ancient Indian Vedic texts dating back to ~1,500 BCE, the chakra system represents a timeless framework for understanding the human energy system.[7]

The word *chakra* comes from Sanskrit and translates to "wheel" or "disk," symbolizing spinning centers of energy within the body. Chakras influence physical, emotional, and spiritual well-being, ensuring the interconnected systems of the body operate in harmony. There are seven primary chakras, each corresponding to different aspects of the human experience, from grounded stability to higher purpose.

What is remarkable about the chakra system is its resonance with modern scientific principles. Concepts such as energy flow, balance, and perception are central to physics, biology, and psychology, bridging the knowledge of the past with the demands of modern leadership. This energetic system is not just confined to the individual; it mirrors the interconnectedness we see throughout nature, science, and society.

Consider the periodic table, where each element plays a unique role in building the structure of the universe. Every element connects to the next, forming an intricate balance essential for life. Similarly, leaders within an organization act as the building blocks of culture and strategy, ensuring that each element of the workforce contributes to the organization's overall stability and growth.

The interconnected nature of energy is also evident in the human nervous system, which acts as a communication network between the brain and the body. Key pathways, such as the vagus nerve, regulate emotional and physical sensations, ensuring the body functions harmoniously. Leaders are the nervous system of their organizations, transmitting vision, clarity, and direction to their teams while maintaining calm and balance during times of stress or uncertainty.

Energy in nature also operates in cycles—the changing seasons, the phases of the moon, and the circadian rhythms that guide our daily lives. Each cycle has a purpose, from rest and renewal to growth and peak activity. Leadership follows a similar rhythm, requiring leaders to balance periods of action with reflection to sustain long-term success.

Finally, consider the vibrations of sound and light, which profoundly shape our experiences of the world. Each chakra resonates with a specific color on the electromagnetic spectrum, from the grounding red of the Root Chakra to the visionary violet of the Crown Chakra. These vibrations remind us that energy is not only present but also measurable, visible, and impactful. Leadership operates in a remarkably similar way. The energy that leaders project—whether it be confidence, compassion, or clarity—creates a ripple effect throughout their organizations, influencing morale, productivity, and innovation. Leaders who align their energy inspire trust, foster connection, and unlock creativity, much like a harmonious symphony in which individual notes combine to create something far greater than the sum of their parts.

The energy of a leader flows in multiple directions: upward to board members and shareholders, downward to employees and teams, and outward to clients and society. This interconnected flow reflects the etymology of the word *corporation*, derived from the Latin *corporare*, meaning "to combine in one body." This linguistic root highlights a fundamental truth: organizations are not just collections of people or processes—they are living, breathing entities that rely on the alignment and vitality of their leaders to thrive.

As we present an understanding of the chakra system, we will intertwine it with three fundamental leadership theories that offer insights into modern leadership. These theories—Transformational Leadership, Servant Leadership, and Emotional Intelligence (EI)—have been carefully chosen because we believe they represent the most impactful and human-centered approaches to effective leadership. Each of these models highlights key leadership qualities, from inspiring vision to fostering trust and building authentic relationships, making them ideal for congruency with the chakra system.

Transformational Leadership was first introduced by James MacGregor Burns in 1978 and later expanded by Bernard M. Bass. It emphasizes the leader's ability to inspire and motivate teams by creating a compelling vision that uplifts both the leader and their followers.[8] Bass identified four core dimensions of transformational leadership:

- **Charisma**: Inspiring admiration and respect by embodying authenticity and purpose.
- **Inspirational Motivation**: Articulating a compelling vision that energizes and unites teams.
- **Intellectual Stimulation**: Encouraging creativity and problem-solving through thought-provoking dialogue.
- **Individualized Consideration**: Acting as a mentor and fostering personal growth and development.[9]

Transformational leadership aligns closely with several chakras, particularly the Solar Plexus Chakra, which governs confidence and personal power, as well as the Crown and Third Eye Chakras, which connect to higher purpose and visionary leadership. Leaders who embody transformational qualities radiate inspiration, confidence, and clarity, guiding their teams with innovation and purpose.

Servant Leadership, introduced by Robert K. Greenleaf in 1970, centers on the idea that a leader's primary role is to serve others. This approach emphasizes empathy, ethical behavior, and the growth and well-being of team members, fostering trust, collaboration, and a culture of care.[10] This leadership style resonates with the Heart Chakra, which governs compassion and connection, and the Root Chakra, which provides stability and a safe foundation. Servant leaders create environments where people thrive, collaboration flourishes, and shared purpose drives performance.

Emotional Intelligence (EI), popularized by Daniel Goleman in the 1990s, emphasizes the importance of recognizing, understanding, and managing both personal emotions and the emotions of others. Goleman identified five key components of EI:

- **Self-Awareness**: Understanding emotional triggers and their impact on decision-making.
- **Self-Regulation**: Maintaining composure and emotional balance in challenging situations.

- **Motivation:** Channeling internal drive to achieve goals and inspire others.
- **Empathy:** Recognizing and responding to the emotional needs of others.
- **Social Skills:** Building trust and strong relationships through effective communication and collaboration.[11]

This aligns with the Throat Chakra, which governs communication, and the Sacral Chakra, which influences emotional flow and interpersonal relationships. Leaders with balanced energy in these areas can foster trust, enhance collaboration, and create emotionally intelligent workplaces.

Just as chakras must remain in balance for physical, emotional, and spiritual well-being, leadership must also be balanced—grounded in purpose, empathetic in action, and clear in communication. Through transformational leadership, leaders inspire. Through servant leadership, they serve. Through EI, they connect. When these styles are viewed through the lens of energetic alignment, they provide an interconnected foundation for understanding how inner balance enables leaders to connect holistically in order to inspire and serve the mind, body, and soul. This enables leaders to create the lasting legacy they desire while fostering growth and well-being across their organizations.

Why Chakras Offer a New Framework for Leadership

How often do you slow down to remind yourself of what the original intention of your organization was, and what it means to be a business leader for the modern world? These days, from the outside, both the leader and their organization can seem strong, have high revenues, experience rapid expansion, and boast an impressive client list. Yet, internally, they sense something is amiss. Morale is slipping. Key employees are burning out. Decision-making feels rushed. This gap between external perception and internal reality is the hallmark of the leadership crisis many executives face today, and it's where the chakra framework offers a new perspective. It is through understanding one's energetic landscape that true transcendence is experienced.

When leaders achieve synergy across all seven chakras—rooted in stability, flowing with creativity, empowered with confidence, leading with compassion, communicating authentically, guided by intuition, and anchored in transcendence—they embody a new paradigm of leadership. They are capable of blending stability with adaptability, empathy with decisiveness, and purpose with practical action.

This energy alignment does more than stave off burnout; it fosters a culture of innovation, trust, and integrity. It is in this collective way of thinking that we can examine the overall singular body of a corporation and how to bring cohesion between all parts of it. Clients, employees, and stakeholders sense the clarity and authenticity that radiate from aligned leadership. As a result, organizations flourish, creating a virtuous cycle of success built on balance and purpose. Good business begets good business—driven by leaders who embody honesty, creativity, and harmony.

However, this is just the beginning. Understanding the chakra system provides a powerful foundation, but true mastery requires a deeper exploration of how each energy center influences leadership, decision-making, and workplace dynamics. Throughout this book, we will go deeper into each specific chakra—what it represents personally and professionally, its connection to leadership science, and how it manifests in both its highest potential and its shadow side.

For each chakra, we will share what it means when its light side is achieved—when it functions in harmony, empowering leaders to lead with authenticity and purpose. Conversely, we will also examine how its shadow side can show up, resulting in an imbalance that may manifest as insecurity, resistance to change, or a disconnect from core values.

Achieving true leadership balance is about more than just mitigating imbalances—it is about integrating energy with practical leadership frameworks to create sustainable, meaningful change. A truly aligned leader is one who leads with strength and compassion, confidence and humility, and intuition and strategy—reflecting an understanding that leadership is not just about managing processes but about nurturing people, fostering innovation, and inspiring lasting impact.

This book offers a roadmap to cultivating that balance, providing tangible tools like an energy meter, techniques, and practices that leaders can implement immediately. Whether it's developing stronger communication through the Throat Chakra, enhancing empathy through the Heart Chakra, or fostering strategic foresight through the Third Eye Chakra, each chapter will offer insights that help leaders step into their full potential.

Ultimately, the journey of CL is one of continual growth, self-discovery, and transformation. It is not a static achievement but an evolving path—one that calls for reflection, awareness, and a willingness to explore the deeper layers of leadership. Leaders who embark on this journey will find themselves not only fostering healthier, more harmonious, and purpose-driven workplaces but also undergoing a profound personal transformation—reconnecting with their sense of purpose, aligning with their values, and cultivating a culture where employees, clients, and stakeholders can truly thrive. This journey invites leaders to move beyond surface-level solutions and embrace a deeper understanding of the energetic forces that influence their leadership style, relationships, and decision-making. It is a path of alignment, balance, and empowerment.

Throughout this book, we will guide you on this experience, exploring each chakra's significance and its direct connection to leadership. Each chapter will discuss:

- The Essence of Each Chakra: Understanding the unique role it plays in both personal and professional realms.
- Connected Leadership Theories: Linking traditional wisdom with modern frameworks such as transformational leadership, servant leadership, and EI.
- The Light and Shadow Sides: Exploring how balanced chakras foster effective leadership while imbalances can manifest as challenges, blind spots, and obstacles.
- Energy Meter: A reflective tool designed to deepen self-awareness, uncover hidden influences, and encourage honest introspection through thought-provoking questions.
- Practical Tools and Techniques: Actionable strategies, mindfulness exercises, and energy-balancing practices designed to bring each chakra into harmony.

By providing this structured approach, the book gives you a comprehensive framework for integrating chakras into leadership in a tangible and practical way. Each chapter serves as a guide to help you identify areas of misalignment, strengthen your energetic foundation, and cultivate a leadership style that is authentic, resilient, and deeply connected to your purpose.

The journey ahead promises to be one of deep transformation—one that will empower you to lead not only with skill and strategy but with a profound sense of inner alignment and connection.

You may have noticed that we've used the word *journey* repeatedly in this chapter. This is no coincidence—every mention is intentional, just as every aspect of this book is designed with purpose. In the following chapters, we will share how some energetic aspects described, including the word "journey," are deeply rooted in Shamanic practices, where leadership has long been regarded as an energetic responsibility. Across cultures and traditions, Shamans have served as guides, bridging the physical and spiritual realms to lead their communities with intuition and a heart-centered approach. Similarly, today's conscious leaders must embrace their roles not just as decision-makers but as stewards of energy, shaping environments that foster connection, creativity, and collective well-being.

Reflecting on the Path Ahead

Leadership is not just about strategy; it's about alignment of the inner self with the external demands of the workplace. As you continue this path of growth and self-discovery, we invite you to take a moment to reflect on how energy influences your leadership and how small, intentional shifts can create profound ripple effects within your organization.

Imagine beginning your day with a sense of stability, feeling rooted and unshaken by external pressures. A simple grounding meditation or a mindful walk could offer that foundation. How stable and secure do you feel as you approach today's challenges?

Envision leading your team with an open heart, fostering trust and genuine connection by starting meetings with authentic expressions of gratitude. How are you cultivating compassion and connection in your leadership?

Consider the power of listening—not just hearing but truly under-standing. In your next conversation, practice active listening, creating space for voices to be fully heard and valued. Are you genuinely valuing the perspectives of those around you?

Before making critical decisions, visualize the ideal outcome and trust your intuition to guide you through uncertainty. Are you balancing strategic thinking with your inner knowing?

These reflections serve as stepping stones on your path to energy-aligned leadership—a journey that begins with self-awareness and extends to creating thriving, balanced organizations.

As you prepare to move forward, consider these key questions to fur-ther introspect where you are today:

- On a scale of 1 to 10, with 10 being highly balanced how balanced is your organization? What factors contribute to this assessment?
- What are the greatest strengths of your leadership? How do these strengths support your organization's goals?
- What are the biggest gaps or areas of need within your leadership?
- How does your organization currently exemplify transformational, servant, and emotionally intelligent leadership?
- What steps can your organization take to cultivate greater balance and alignment?

This is just the beginning, and with each step, you will uncover new insights, deepen your self-awareness, and harness the power of energetic alignment to lead with authenticity, resilience, and purpose. Consider this book as a guide that can be integrated holistically into your personal leadership style and business, but also as an oracle book. If there is one specific area that you feel is out of balance, you can open directly to that chapter and receive the insight you need to bring yourself, your team, or your organization back into balance. Conversely, if you are looking for sudden inspiration in an area that can be optimized in the moment, allow yourself to close your eyes and open to a page at random. The words you receive are those that are meant to help you as a leader at that time. When the lessons, questions, and dialectics are taken with intention, the result is a shift in your own energy as a leader, how your embodiment inspires your employees, and how the corporation rises in abundance as the shining example for consciously aligned business.

Take a deep breath. Step forward with intention. Allow the journey to unfold.

References

1. Fortune. (n.d.). *Fortune 500*. Retrieved December, 2024, from https://fortune.com/ranking/fortune500/
2. Forbes. (n.d.). *Forbes Global 2000*. Retrieved December, 2024, from https://www.forbes.com/lists/global2000/
3. Harter, J. (2022, September 6). *Is quiet quitting real?* Gallup. Retrieved from https://www.gallup.com/workplace/398306/quiet-quitting-real.aspx
4. Henson, W. (2023, June 5). *Industrial revolution hangovers, part I: Corporate hierarchy*. Forbes. Retrieved from https://www.forbes.com/sites/forbesbooksauthors/2023/06/05/industrial-revolution-hangovers-part-i-corporate-hierarchy/
5. Harvard Business School. (n.d.). *The Hawthorne studies*. Retrieved from https://www.library.hbs.edu/hc/hawthorne/09.html
6. Soren, A., & Ryff, C. D. (2023). Meaningful work, well-being, and health: Enacting a Eudaimonic vision. *International Journal of Environmental Research and Public Health*, 20(16), 6570. https://doi.org/10.3390/ijerph20166570
7. Cooper, N. J. (2020). *A brief history of the chakras in the human body*. ResearchGate. Retrieved from https://www.researchgate.net/profile/Nj-Cooper-2/publication/342562977_A_Brief_History_of_the_Chakras_in_Human_Body/links/5efb5246299bf18816f398d2/A-Brief-History-of-the-Chakras-in-Human-Body.pdf
8. Burns, J. M. (1978). *Leadership*. Harper & Row.
9. Bass, B. M. (1985). *Leadership and Performance beyond Expectations*. Free Press; Collier Macmillan.
10. Greenleaf, R. K. (1977). *Servant leadership: A journey into the nature of legitimate power and greatness*. Paulist Press.
11. Goleman, D. (1995). *Emotional intelligence: Why it can matter more than IQ*. Bantam Books.

Chapter 1

Chakras and Leadership
A New Paradigm

Source: iStock.com/Jorm Sangsorn

Our Journey

When someone refers to you as a leader, the immediate association often revolves around the title you hold, the authority you command, and the influence you exert. However, true leadership transcends titles and responsibilities—it is an energy, an intention, and a presence that permeates every aspect of an organization. It is the unseen force that shapes culture, drives innovation, and inspires others to move toward a shared vision with purpose and clarity.

Today, leadership demands more than strategic thinking and decision-making; it requires an understanding of self-leadership. Before a leader can effectively guide others, they must first cultivate inner clarity and stability. An analogy to illustrate this concept is the familiar instruction given during airline safety briefings: put on your oxygen mask first before assisting others. As a leader, managing your own physical presence,

DOI: 10.4324/9781003635918-2

emotions, thoughts, and energy is not a luxury—it is a necessity. Your energy becomes the undercurrent that your team absorbs, particularly in moments of high stakes or crisis. Hence, personal energy management becomes one of the most valuable tools a modern leader can cultivate. The ability to maintain a calm and centered disposition—whether navigating adrenaline-charged decisions, billion-dollar mergers, or critical product launches—distinguishes truly embodied leadership. Leaders who master their energy create an aura of stability, resilience, and focus within their organizations, offering a powerful foundation for sustained success and growth.

Neal's Journey: Energy Management in High-Stakes Leadership

For years, Neal thrived in the fast-paced world of Wall Street, working on the Leveraged and Structured Finance Capital Markets and Syndicate desk at Goldman Sachs. Days were filled with ringing phones, simultaneous deals in the market, looming deadlines, and the constant pressure of billion-dollar transactions underwritten on the firm's balance sheet. It was common for analysts and managing directors alike to ask Neal, *"How do you remain so calm all the time?"*

The truth was that the high-pressure environment could have easily consumed Neal, but he had an anchor—something he had learned early in life. From the age of five, Neal was introduced to yogic meditation techniques, a practice that had once been a distant memory during his early career hustle. However, as his job demands escalated, he returned to these practices and they transformed the way he navigated the relentless pace of investment banking.

By integrating meditation, mindfulness, and knowledge of the chakra system, he was able to slow down his internal stress while increasing his external output. Neal discovered that when energy is managed effectively, productivity skyrockets—not through frantic multitasking but through focused, intentional effort.

Energy management is the key to efficiency. It's the difference between operating at 10% focus for 100% of the time versus 100% focus in just 10% of the time. When individuals cultivate energetic awareness, focused presence, and conscious boundaries, they evolve into resilient, high-performing leaders.

Returning to mindfulness and energy practices allowed Neal to approach work with greater clarity, adaptability, and a sense of calm—even in the face of tight deadlines, complex negotiations, and high-stakes decisions. This balance not only enhanced his well-being but also created an atmosphere of confidence and reliability within his teams.

Zohra's Journey: A Legacy of Healing and Leadership

Growing up in a family of healers, Zohra was immersed in the power of energy and intention from an early age. Her home was filled with conversations about balance, transformation, and the unseen forces that guide our well-being. Though the healers in her family have since passed, their legacy continues to inspire her, leading her to explore the profound intersection between ancient wisdom and leadership in the modern world.

This curiosity led her to pursue yoga teacher training (Yin/Hatha), deepening her understanding of the body's subtle energy systems. Over time, her journey expanded to include Shamanic training/practices, where she discovered how energy alignment and holistic healing play an essential role in effective leadership.

Zohra's academic pursuits complemented these spiritual teachings. With a doctorate in education, leadership, and learning, she began to bridge energetic practices with modern leadership science, studying how leaders grow, adapt, and thrive in complex environments. Through this integration, it became clear that chakras offer a framework to decode leadership behaviors—whether it's a leader struggling with micromanagement due to an unbalanced Root Chakra or a lack of vision stemming from an underactive Third Eye Chakra.

Chakra Leadership

If leadership is not about being in charge, but rather taking care of those in your charge (as Simon Sinek reminds us), then how can a leader take care of their team if they haven't first taken care of themselves?

A leader's energy sets the tone for their entire organization. Whether they walk into a room with calm assurance or bring the weight of stress and exhaustion with them, their energy ripples outward, influencing morale, decision-making, and performance at every level. This is why energy management is no longer just a personal endeavor; it is an organizational imperative.

Many leaders today feel the strain of split attention, juggling responsibilities while trying to maintain focus and presence. It's easy to pour everything into work—meeting after meeting, decision after decision—until there's nothing left to give. In the end, you can't pour from an empty cup. If you're operating on empty, struggling with exhaustion and imbalance, how can you hope to inspire, guide, and support others effectively? The truth is, you can only serve others fully when your own energy is overflowing with abundant wholeness.

This is where CL introduces a new way forward. We define CL as the science of analyzing one's own energy centers in order to bring coherent alignment within. In doing so, leaders can show up with greater authenticity, compassion, and effectiveness. This form of leadership science acknowledges the duality of overactive and underactive energy centers while emphasizing strengths and transmuting shadow aspects of leadership linked to energy imbalances. CL offers a transformative lens through which leaders can understand their own energetic landscape—bridging the physical, emotional, mental, and spiritual aspects of leadership into one cohesive whole.

Consider a leader who's just completed a marathon day of back-to-back meetings. They walk out feeling physically drained, their posture slouched, and a headache creeping in. The emotional energy lingers too—perhaps the frustration from a tense discussion or the disappointment of an unmet expectation. Soon, these feelings begin to weigh on their mental state, replaying moments of the day over and over again, making it difficult to focus on what's next or their own home and personal life.

This cascade effect—where physical exhaustion impacts emotional well-being and clouds mental clarity—is not unusual. It happens all the time. Yet, few leaders stop to recognize how interconnected these energy layers truly are. When mismanaged, they lead to reactive decision-making, disengagement, and a growing sense of disconnection—from both the team and themselves. But imagine if that same leader, instead of pushing through exhaustion, took a moment to realign their energy—grounding themselves through breathwork, releasing emotional tension, and finding mental clarity through a brief moment of stillness. Suddenly, the day feels more manageable, and they're able to walk into the next conversation with renewed presence. This is the essence of CL: a conscious, energetic approach to self-leadership that impacts every level of an organization.

Why Energy Matters in Leadership

CL is about more than just self-care; it is a strategic tool that enables leaders to show up as their best selves *consistently*. It involves understanding the body's seven primary energy centers—each representing different aspects of leadership—and bringing them into alignment (aka balance) to enhance vitality. Exploring one's emotional landscape, mental patterns, and spiritual self becomes the fertile soil from which CL takes root, creating impactful and tangible changes in their work, relationships, and life. Understanding the energetic system within matters because when a leader's energy is aligned, they are able to:

- Lead with clarity and confidence, making decisions from a place of balance rather than burnout.
- Foster authentic connection, ensuring their presence uplifts and inspires their teams.
- Navigate high-pressure situations with composure and emotional resilience.

However, when these energy centers are out of balance, it shows up in often unnoticed, but significantly impactful behaviors. In energetic terms, we call it misaligned energy, and it can manifest in several ways, leading to common leadership challenges, such as, micromanagement and control (Root Chakra imbalance), emotional detachment (Heart Chakra imbalance), poor communication (Throat Chakra imbalance), and lack of vision (Third Eye Chakra imbalance). These imbalances often go unaddressed in traditional leadership models, which tend to focus on skills and strategies rather than the energy that drives them. As the internal challenges go unnoticed, it leads to a reactive cycle that further manifests into exhaustion and fatigue. However, CL offers a more sustainable, conscious approach and helps leaders shift from surviving to thriving by providing a framework for:

1 **Self-Awareness**: Understanding personal energy patterns and how they influence leadership.
2 **Alignment**: Bringing balance to the physical, emotional, mental, and spiritual layers of leadership.
3 **Intentional Leadership**: Leading with clarity, purpose, and authenticity rather than reacting to pressures.

So, how does one gauge energetic alignment within oneself, and how can that ultimately correlate to the organization they lead? Billionaire Founder and CEO of Amazon, Jeff Bezos, offered his own perspective on energy management when he stated during a live Q&A, "Usually it's about: do you have energy, and is your work depriving you of energy or is your work generating energy for you?" Bezos highlights a fundamental truth—work should not be a constant drain, but rather a source of alignment and fulfillment that generates energy. When leaders are in coherent alignment with their values, they are able to show up with passion, purpose, and resilience.

But how can leaders assess their own energy levels and alignment? Fortunately, recent advancements in technology are providing tangible ways to measure and visualize energetic states. Tools such as the Bio-Well, developed by Dr. Konstantin Korotkov, utilize Gas Discharge Visualization (GDV) or Electro-Photonic Imaging (EPI) to conduct human energy scans. You can even catch a glimpse of that device in action on the first episode of the Amazon Prime series titled "Bliss-Up." Using the device, a weak electrical current is applied to the fingertip for less than a millisecond, prompting an emission of electrons that excite air molecules. The resulting gas discharge glow is captured by a video camera and processed by sophisticated software, generating a comprehensive analysis of a person's energy field.[1] These scans provide insights into:

- Energy field balance
- Chakra alignment
- Organ stress levels
- Biorhythms and Meridian system evaluation

While technological advancements offer fascinating insights into energy alignment, the most powerful and accessible tool for assessing energetic balance lies within the human body itself. Our bodies constantly communicate with us through subtle cues—whether it's the tension in our chest before a difficult conversation, the fatigue in our limbs after a long day, or the racing thoughts that prevent us from being fully present. These sensations are not just physical responses; they are signals of deeper energetic imbalances that, if left unaddressed, can manifest as stress, indecisiveness, or emotional detachment in leadership. Yes, our bodies truly keep score. However, tuning into these signals requires creating space—space to be fully present with one's thoughts, emotions, and physical sensations. This practice of stillness and awareness opens the doorway to greater self-understanding, helping leaders identify misalignments before they escalate into burnout or disconnection. In a world that constantly demands action and reaction, the ability to pause, reflect, and realign is a critical leadership skill.

To cultivate greater energetic self-awareness, leaders can engage in simple reflective practices that promote a deeper connection with their inner selves. These include:

- **Journaling**: Regular reflection through writing allows leaders to identify recurring emotional patterns and mental themes—whether in personal or professional life. This process provides clarity on what energizes them and what depletes them, offering insights into necessary shifts.
- **Meditation**: Stepping away from the noise and entering a meditative state enables leaders to tap into their inner knowing and intuition. Meditation strengthens self-awareness, offering moments of clarity that can lead to better decision-making and emotional resilience.

- **Body Scanning**: A guided or self-directed practice of scanning the body from head to toe with focused attention on each chakra can reveal areas of tension, warmth, or stagnation. This conscious observation helps leaders recognize where they may be holding stress and how it connects to their leadership presence.

For those new to these practices, exploring one's energetic dimensions may seem unfamiliar at first. However, just like mastering a professional skill, personal energy management is a discipline that grows stronger with conscious and consistent practice.

Leadership Science and Chakras Unify

Across various leadership models, the importance of maintaining balance—mentally, emotionally, and physically—emerges as a recurring theme, proving that effective leadership is deeply tied to one's ability to manage their internal state. Rather than being static, leadership energy moves fluidly between balance, underactivity, and overactivity much like underutilized or overutilized resources in a business. Imagine a horizontal spectrum with underactive energy at one end, overactive energy at the other, and balance in the center. When a chakra is underactive, leadership energy becomes diminished or blocked. Leaders may experience indecisiveness, lack of motivation, and emotional detachment, leading to disengaged teams and a stagnant work environment. They may avoid challenges, struggle to assert authority, or lack the drive to move projects forward effectively. On the other end of the spectrum, overactive energy can result in excessive control, micromanagement, and emotional volatility. Leaders in this state may find themselves overwhelmed, over-involved, or constantly reacting to situations rather than leading proactively. This can create tension within teams, foster burnout, and lead to a culture of fear rather than empowerment. The key to effective leadership is learning to recognize where you fall on this spectrum and continuously recalibrating to return to a state of balance. When chakras are in balance, leaders feel empowered. They cultivate an environment of psychological safety, spark innovation, and inspire their teams to pursue shared goals with enthusiasm and purpose—without succumbing to exhaustion or frustration.

By applying the chakra framework, leaders can move beyond vague feelings of being off or burned out and instead develop a clear understanding of where their energy may need recalibration. As such, leaders who consciously cultivate their energetic alignment are better equipped to stay grounded and resilient during challenges, communicate with clarity and authenticity, inspire creativity and innovation, and build meaningful connections that foster trust and collaboration. Bringing the understanding of chakras into the modern workplace allows leaders to peel back the onion to know themselves on the deepest layers. They begin to understand the intention behind each decision, and if it comes from a genuine place of service, empathy, and divine inspiration. When this is achieved, leaders then have the capacity to genuinely take care of themselves, and in turn, those in their charge.

Reflection and the Path to Chakra Leadership

Leadership is an ongoing adventure—one that's less about achieving perfection and more about navigating the twists and turns with self-awareness and intentional energy. Achieving energetic alignment isn't about ticking boxes; it's about making space for reflection as we lead.

As we move forward in this book, let's first create the space and time for thoughtful reflection. Consider the following concepts through the lens of your existing knowledge, channel your energy into your leadership journey, and deepen your leadership practice. By the end of this chapter, you will also find a table designed to serve as a practical guide, helping you bridge your current understanding of the chakra system with contemporary leadership frameworks. Use this guide to recognize areas where your leadership energy may require recalibration, reflect on your strengths and areas for growth, and apply practical strategies to cultivate deeper alignment in both your personal and professional journey. Whether your goal is to build stability, foster authentic communication, or develop a compelling vision, this table offers valuable insights to help you lead with purpose, confidence, and balance.

Grounding Stability (Root Chakra and Servant Leadership)

Imagine starting your day feeling steady and secure, regardless of the challenges ahead. Taking just a few minutes each morning to breathe deeply and visualize roots anchoring you to the earth can foster a profound sense of stability.

- **Reflection**: How do you handle uncertainty or high-pressure situations?

Fostering Compassion and Connection (Heart Chakra and Servant Leadership)

Leadership is fundamentally about connection—demonstrating care and empathy while maintaining healthy boundaries. A simple practice like expressing gratitude can strengthen relationships and build trust within your team.

- **Reflection:** How do you nurture compassion and emotional connection in your leadership?

Authentic Communication (Throat Chakra and Emotional Intelligence)

Communication serves as the bridge between vision and execution. Active listening—being fully present without interruption—opens new channels of trust and clarity within your organization.

- **Reflection:** Do you express your ideas clearly, and do you actively listen to others?

Vision and Intuition (Third Eye Chakra and Transformational Leadership)

When it comes to key decisions, both intuition and a higher sense of purpose play vital roles. The Third Eye Chakra governs insight, strategic foresight, and the ability to see beyond immediate challenges, while the Crown Chakra connects leaders to a higher purpose, inspiring them to align their vision with long-term goals. Taking a quiet moment to visualize the ideal outcome, trust your inner compass, and align decisions with a greater mission can provide the clarity and confidence needed to lead with authenticity and purpose.

- **Reflection:** How do you balance trusting your intuition with strategic planning?
- **Reflection:** How do I align my leadership with a higher purpose?

These small yet intentional practices create the foundation for **balanced, conscious leadership.** As you reflect, consider the following questions to gain ongoing insights into your leadership energy:

- How have you been managing your energy as a leader?
- How does your personal energy affect your team and organization?
- What areas of your leadership feel balanced, and where do you notice misalignment?
- What tangible steps can you take to create greater harmony in your leadership?

The journey toward energy-aligned leadership is not about quick fixes, it's about cultivating long-term habits. Each step you take toward aligning your energy is a step toward transforming not only yourself but also the

Chakra	Leadership Trait	Leadership Model	Reflection Question	Suggested Practice
Root (Grounding)	Stability and Security	Servant Leadership	How do I handle uncertainty or pressure?	Morning grounding meditation or a mindful walk
Sacral (Creativity)	Emotional Intelligence	Emotional Intelligence	How do I foster creativity and collaboration?	Encouraging team brainstorming and self-expression exercises
Solar Plexus (Confidence)	Purpose and Empowerment	Transformational Leadership	How do I inspire and empower my team?	Setting clear intentions and affirmations
Heart (Compassion)	Connection and Trust	Servant Leadership	How do I show care and empathy while maintaining boundaries?	Expressing gratitude and active listening
Throat (Communication)	Authentic Expression	Emotional Intelligence	How often do I communicate openly and authentically?	Practicing active listening and honest feedback
Third Eye (Vision)	Intuition and Strategic Foresight	Transformational Leadership	How do I balance intuition with strategic planning?	Visualization exercises for key decision-making
Crown (Purpose)	Higher Insight and Values	Transformational Leadership	How do I align my leadership with a higher purpose?	Meditation and reflective journaling on long-term vision

culture of your organization. As we continue through this book, we will share each chakra in greater depth, uncovering its connection to leadership and offering practical strategies for achieving greater balance and alignment. This journey is not just about understanding concepts—it's about embodying them. True leadership starts from within, and the path to illuminating that inner light is yours to walk first; from there, you empower others.

Reference

1. Korotkov, K. (2002). *Measuring energy fields: State of the science.* Backbone Publishing.

Chapter 2

The Chakra System

An Energetic Framework for Leadership

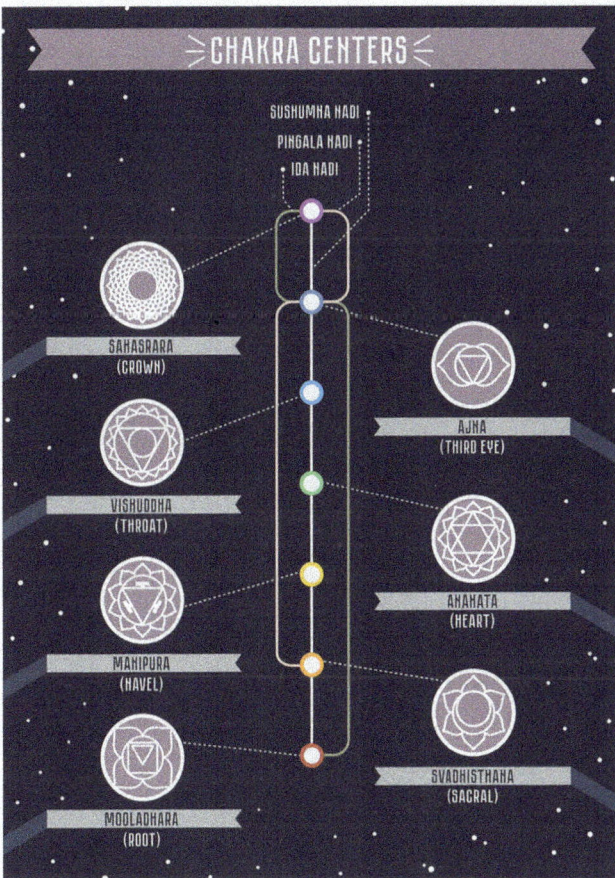

Source: iStock.com/OlgaKN

DOI: 10.4324/9781003635918-3

The Role of Chakras in Personal and Professional Lives

Throughout our journeys—one rooted in Shamanic practices and the other in angelic guidance and spiritual connection—we have come to understand that energy alignment shapes not just personal growth but also leadership potential. Our work has brought us into close proximity with leaders across industries—executives, entrepreneurs, and changemakers—who were caught in the relentless rhythm of moving from one challenge to the next. We observed a common pattern—leaders driven by ego, ambition, and external validation, tirelessly pushing forward without pausing to reflect on their own state of being. This constant striving for more—more success, more recognition, more growth—often led to a sense of emptiness and lack of fulfillment within their organizations and teams. These experiences revealed a profound truth: leadership without energetic alignment empties the organization of its essence.

The human connections—the heartbeat of any successful enterprise—become secondary to sterile Key Performance Indicators (KPIs) and metrics. When organizations feel hollow, employees disengage, innovation slows, and turnover increases. The focus shifts away from collaboration and inspiration to survival and apathy. This journey toward energetic alignment does not negate ambition or diminish the pursuit of excellence. Rather, it enables leaders to harness their energy intentionally to create cultures of well-being which extend beyond the bottom line. Through this understanding, we have come to see leadership not just as a role, but as an energetic responsibility. The energy leaders carry—whether conscious or unconscious—move through their teams, shaping morale, comradery, and organizational success.

Leadership rooted in energetic awareness not only transforms the individual leader but also breathes life back into the organization, reigniting purpose and creating a thriving, inspired community. We saw and learned how grounding through the Root Chakra builds resilience, how the Heart Chakra fosters connection and empathy, and how the Crown Chakra inspires a sense of higher purpose and visionary leadership, to name a few. These insights aren't just theoretical—they stem from our personal and professional experiences. Whether navigating complex challenges in the workplace or seeking deeper spiritual alignment, balancing our energy centers has allowed us to show up with greater intention in all life situations.

Energy Flow and Its Impact on Leadership Effectiveness

The chakra system can be thought of as the dashboard of our energy, providing critical signals about our internal states—just as dashboard lights in a car indicate where attention is needed to maintain peak performance. Whether it's an oil change, tire rotation, or engine check, each issue requires a unique solution to restore balance and ensure the vehicle runs smoothly. Similarly, our human energy system operates much the same way. In leadership, these energetic indicators often manifest as stress, burnout, communication breakdowns, or a lack of clarity and vision. Ignoring these signals can lead to reactive decision-making and a leadership style that feels stuck or uninspired.

This is where the chakra system offers guidance into leadership and personal growth. Each chakra illuminates different dimensions of leadership qualities and challenges alongside different aspects of life, nature, and leadership. Traditionally depicted as lotus flowers with a distinct number of petals, each chakra corresponds to a unique color—mirroring the colors of the rainbow—and represents specific energies that influence our physical, emotional, and spiritual well-being. As we mentioned in Chapter 1, a leader's energy can manifest in three ways along the energy spectrum, especially in leadership:

- **Balanced (Optimal Performance)**: The leadership energy is in harmony, allowing for clear decision-making, steady confidence, and an empowering leadership presence. Balanced energy fosters trust, innovation, and sustainable growth.
- **Underactive (Insufficient Energy)**: The leadership energy is blocked or diminished, leading to hesitation, lack of confidence, and disengagement. Leaders may struggle with decision-making, feel overwhelmed, and fail to inspire their teams.
- **Overactive (Excessive Energy)**: The leadership energy becomes overwhelming, resulting in micromanagement, emotional reactivity, and a controlling leadership style that stifles creativity and autonomy within the team.

Chakra System: An Overview

We continue to hear people, especially leaders, say, "*I feel something is off*"; yet few can articulate exactly what that "off" is. In boardrooms, executive retreats, and leadership forums, the language of energy is emerging—words like flow, alignment, and intuition are becoming part

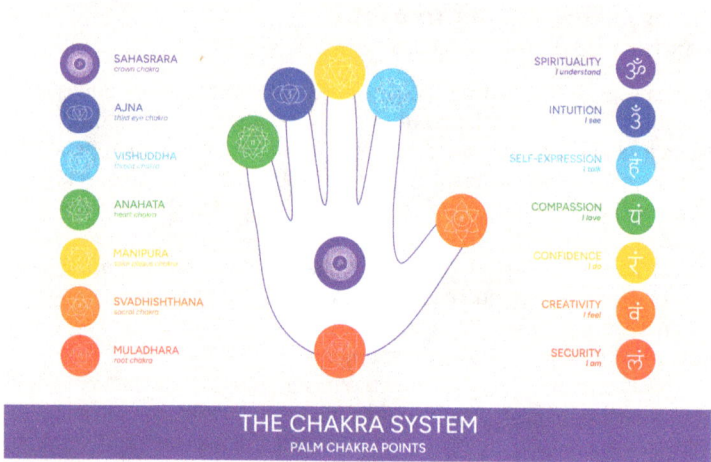

THE CHAKRA SYSTEM
PALM CHAKRA POINTS

Source: iStock.com/LiiaLonnArt

of daily conversations. But despite this growing awareness, many leaders still lack a structured vocabulary and practical toolkit to understand their internal imbalances and how to truly address them. We believe it is time to offer leaders a deeper understanding of what is happening within them—a roadmap to recognize, articulate, and balance their own energy.

For millennia, the chakra system has served as the backbone of Indian spirituality, yoga practices, and energetic healing systems. Across the globe, many ancient cultures have recognized the presence of a universal life force energy that animates all living things and connects them to a higher consciousness. This basic concept of life force is known by many names—Prana in India, Chi (Qi) in China, Ki in Japan, Orenda among the Haudenosaunee, Mana in Polynesia, Sekhem (Ka) in ancient Egypt, Pneuma in Greece, Ruach in Hebrew traditions, and Ashe among the Yoruba of West Africa. These cultures believe that there is a crucial life force behind the existence of animate life on Earth. Despite cultural differences and slight permutations, the recognition of this vital energy has transcended time and geography, shaping the way humans perceive their connection to themselves and the world around them.

In the chakra system, this flow of energy moves along the spinal axis, from the coccyx (tailbone, Root Chakra) to the medulla oblongata, and ultimately exits through the crown of the head via the Crown Chakra. When energy flows without stagnation, individuals experience clarity, resilience, and inspiration; however, when it becomes obstructed, symptoms of imbalance—such as fatigue, indecision, and disconnection—begin to surface. In many ways, leadership mirrors this energetic flow.[1] Just as energy must flow freely from the Root to the Crown for balance and well-being, effective leadership must be grounded in stability before it can evolve into a higher vision and purpose. To fully grasp the connection between chakras and leadership, let's first understand the distinct qualities governed by each energy center.

The Root Chakra

The first chakra is the Root Chakra. It is located at the base of the spine, represented by the color red with four petals, and is associated with the element of earth. It signifies grounding, stability, group identity, and safety. In leadership, this translates to establishing a secure foundation—fostering an environment of psychological safety, trust, and strong core values that ground an organization. Energetically, a leader may show up as:

- **Balanced Root Chakra**: Leaders exude confidence, resilience, and the ability to navigate uncertainty with steadiness and assurance. Their grounded presence provides a sense of security, empowering their teams to take risks and grow.
- **Underactive Root Chakra**: Leaders may experience insecurity, indecision, and fear of change, resulting in a lack of clear direction and an unstable work environment.
- **Overactive Root Chakra**: Leaders might exhibit excessive control and rigidity, micromanaging their teams and resisting change due to an overwhelming need for security and control.

The Sacral Chakra

The second chakra is the Sacral Chakra. It is located just below the navel, depicted as orange with six petals, and is associated with the element of water. It governs creativity, EI, adaptability, and the ability to form meaningful relationships. Just as water flows effortlessly and takes the shape of its container, leaders who embody the energy of the Sacral Chakra can adapt to change with grace, nurture collaboration, and foster a culture of creativity and emotional connection. Energetically, a leader may show up as:

- **Balanced Sacral Chakra:** Leaders are emotionally aware, empathetic, and open to diverse ideas, creating workplaces where creativity flourishes, collaboration is effortless, and innovation thrives. They understand that leadership is not just about strategy but also about building meaningful relationships and fostering an environment of emotional safety.
- **Underactive Sacral Chakra:** Leaders may struggle with emotional repression, rigidity, and fear of change. This can lead to difficulty in forming meaningful connections, a lack of creative thinking, and resistance to new ideas.
- **Overactive Sacral Chakra:** Leaders may become overly emotional, reactive, or dependent on external validation. This can result in blurred professional boundaries, favoritism, and inconsistency in decision-making.

The Solar Plexus Chakra

The third chakra is the Solar Plexus Chakra. It is located in the upper abdomen, symbolized by a yellow lotus with ten petals, and is associated with the element of fire. This energy center is deeply connected to lessons of personal power, self-esteem, confidence, and leadership authenticity. It is the driving force behind our willpower, motivation, and ability to take decisive action—essentially, it represents honoring oneself and one's true potential. Energetically, a leader may show up as:

- **Balanced Solar Plexus Chakra:** Leaders exude confidence, inspire their teams with clarity and purpose, and empower others to achieve ambitious goals. They strike a balance between assertiveness and humility, leading with strength and compassion.
- **Underactive Solar Plexus Chakra:** Leaders may lack confidence in their abilities, struggle with decision-making, and experience self-doubt, leading to hesitation and inaction.
- **Overactive Solar Plexus Chakra:** Leaders may exhibit controlling tendencies, micromanagement, and an excessive focus on personal achievements, often seeking constant validation at the expense of their team's well-being.

The Heart Chakra

The fourth chakra is the Heart Chakra. The Heart Chakra, traditionally represented by a green lotus with 12 petals, is associated with the element of air and governs compassion, empathy, and authentic connection.

Positioned at the center of the chakra system, it acts as a bridge between the lower three chakras, which are connected to the physical world, and the upper three chakras, which align with spiritual awareness. This energy center embodies profound lessons in love, forgiveness, and healing, reminding us that true leadership is rooted in the ability to lead with heart-centered integrity. Energetically, a leader may show up as:

- **Balanced Heart Chakra**: Leaders foster trust, loyalty, and a sense of belonging within their teams by demonstrating empathy, kindness, and EI. They create inclusive, emotionally safe workplaces that inspire collaboration.
- **Underactive Heart Chakra**: Leaders may appear distant, detached, or indifferent, struggling to connect emotionally with their teams, leading to low morale and disengagement.
- **Overactive Heart Chakra**: Leaders may overextend themselves emotionally, struggle with setting boundaries, and take on too much responsibility, leading to burnout and inefficiency.

The Throat Chakra

Moving higher along the spinal axis, the fifth chakra is the Throat Chakra. Depicted as a light blue lotus with 16 petals, it is linked to the element of ether (sound). It serves as the center of communication and self-expression, representing the ability to speak our truth and articulate ideas. Effective leaders recognize that communication is not just about speaking but also about active listening, engaging in meaningful dialogue, and fostering an environment where others feel heard and valued. Leaders who embody the essence of the Throat Chakra possess the willpower and conviction to articulate their vision with authenticity, inspiring trust and alignment within their organizations. Energetically, a leader may show up as:

- **Balanced Throat Chakra**: Leaders communicate with clarity, confidence, and transparency, fostering a culture of trust and open dialogue. They encourage meaningful discussions and ensure that their vision and values are understood across the organization.
- **Underactive Throat Chakra**: Leaders may struggle to express their thoughts, avoid difficult conversations, and experience difficulty in asserting their ideas, leading to confusion and a lack of direction.
- **Overactive Throat Chakra**: Leaders may dominate conversations, over-explain, or struggle with listening, creating an environment where others feel unheard or undervalued.

The Third-Eye Chakra

The sixth chakra is the Third Eye Chakra. It is located at the point between the eyebrows, symbolized by an indigo lotus with two petals, and connected to the element of light. This energy center governs intuition, insight, and strategic foresight. It is the gateway to higher awareness, enabling leaders to perceive beyond immediate challenges and anticipate long-term opportunities. This energy center encourages leaders to move beyond reactive decision-making and cultivate a proactive, strategic mindset that drives innovation and sustainable growth. Energetically, a leader may show up as:

- **Balanced Third Eye Chakra:** Leaders have strong intuitive abilities, make insightful decisions, and balance logical thinking with creative vision, driving innovation and long-term success.
- **Underactive Third Eye Chakra:** Leaders may struggle with indecisiveness, short-term thinking, and an over-reliance on data without trusting their instincts, leading to missed opportunities.
- **Overactive Third Eye Chakra:** Leaders may become too focused on visionary thinking, disconnected from practical realities, or prone to overanalyzing situations without taking action.

The Crown Chakra

At the very top of the energetic system sits the Crown Chakra, the seventh chakra. Depicted as a 1,000-petaled lotus and connected to divine consciousness, presence, and higher purpose. This chakra represents the highest state of awareness, where leaders align their personal values with their organizational mission, acting from a place of integrity, inspiration, and service to the greater good. By aligning this energy center, leaders cultivate a sense of spiritual clarity and inner alignment, guiding their organizations with wisdom, purpose, and an unwavering commitment to their core values. Energetically, a leader may show up as:

- **Balanced Crown Chakra:** Leaders operate with a profound sense of purpose, aligning their work with ethical values, and inspiring their teams with a shared mission and vision for the future. They see leadership as a service to a greater cause beyond profits and productivity.
- **Underactive Crown Chakra:** Leaders may feel disconnected from their purpose, uninspired, and focused only on day-to-day tasks, lacking a broader sense of direction.
- **Overactive Crown Chakra:** Leaders may become overly idealistic, detached from operational realities, or disconnected from their teams, leading to impractical strategies and a lack of grounded execution.

Whether you're seeking to cultivate stability and trust through the Root Chakra, harness creativity and collaboration with the Sacral Chakra, or lead with vision and higher purpose via the Crown Chakra, the chakra system offers a tangible roadmap for growth and transformation. To support your journey in balancing leadership energy, the following table serves as a handy reference guide. It provides a quick overview of how each chakra aligns with core leadership attributes, helping you identify growth opportunities, address potential imbalances, and create a leadership style rooted in holistic awareness and effectiveness.

How to Use This Table

Use this table to identify where you might be experiencing imbalances—whether feeling uninspired, lacking direction, or experiencing over-control. Recognizing these patterns allows you to take intentional steps toward recalibrating your energy, fostering greater resilience, and leading with authenticity.

Chakra System: The Interconnectedness

While the chakras are vertically aligned along the spine, they do not function in isolation. Instead, they operate as an interconnected system, influencing and supporting one another in a delicate balance. Each chakra holds a unique function—whether it's grounding (Root Chakra), EI (Sacral Chakra), or visionary thinking (Third Eye Chakra)—but their true power lies in their synergy. Similarly, as a well-functioning organization requires collaboration across departments, the energy flow within our bodies depends on the harmonious interaction of all chakras. When one chakra is out of balance, its influence cascades to the others, creating a ripple effect that impacts our holistic well-being. For example, if the Root Chakra, which provides stability and security, is weak, it may lead to a lack of confidence and indecisiveness in the Solar Plexus Chakra, which governs personal power and leadership authority. Conversely, an overactive Solar Plexus without the grounding influence of the Root Chakra may result in ego-driven leadership that lacks empathy and connection.

In leadership, this interconnectedness mirrors the complexities of managing an organization. A leader cannot focus solely on one aspect of their role—such as strategy—without considering the emotional and cultural well-being of their team. A leader's ability to inspire vision (Crown Chakra) must be supported by clear communication (Throat Chakra), emotional connection (Heart Chakra), and decisive action (Solar Plexus Chakra). If any of these areas are misaligned, the overall effectiveness of

Chakra Name	Property	Color	Location	Balanced Leadership Traits	Underactive Leadership Traits	Overactive Leadership Traits
Root Chakra	Grounding and Stability	Red	Base of Spine	Provides stability, trust, and reliability	Fear-driven decision-making, insecurity, and lack of trust	Micromanagement, resistance to change, and excessive control
Sacral Chakra	Creativity and Emotional Flow	Orange	Below Navel	Encourages creativity, adaptability, and emotional connection	Emotional stagnation and difficulty forming relationships	Over-dependence on validation and emotional volatility
Solar Plexus Chakra	Confidence and Personal Power	Yellow	Upper Abdomen	Leads with confidence, decisiveness, and empowerment	Hesitation, low self-esteem, and lack of direction	Over-controlling tendencies, arrogance, and a need for dominance
Heart Chakra	Compassion and Connection	Green	Center of Chest	Fosters empathy, trust, and inclusive relationships	Emotional detachment and difficulty forming connections	Over-involvement, inability to set healthy boundaries
Throat Chakra	Communication and Authenticity	Blue	Throat	Communicates with authenticity and transparency	Avoidance of difficult conversations, fear of self-expression	Over-communication, dominating conversations, and a lack of listening
Third Eye Chakra	Intuition and Vision	Indigo	Between Eyebrows	Offers clear vision, insight, and strategic guidance	Lack of clarity, indecisiveness, and poor intuition	Over-reliance on intuition and disconnection from reality
Crown Chakra	Purpose and Higher Insight	Violet	Top of Head	Inspires purpose, ethical leadership, and alignment with values	Disconnection from purpose and feeling uninspired	Over-idealism, impracticality, and detachment from reality

leadership diminishes. Think of the chakra system as a symphony orchestra—each instrument (or chakra) has its unique sound and purpose, yet when played in harmony with others, it creates a masterpiece. A violin may carry the melody, but it relies on the steady rhythm of the percussion and the depth of the bass to create a complete experience. Similarly, leadership requires a synchronized approach, where foundational stability (Root Chakra) supports confident decision-making (Solar Plexus Chakra) and clear communication (Throat Chakra) enhances visionary leadership (Crown Chakra). If one instrument is out of tune, the entire orchestra feels its impact—just as an imbalance in one chakra can disrupt a leader's overall effectiveness.

The interconnectedness of chakras is not limited to balance and imbalance states. An added layer to chakras that leaders must also recognize is the dynamic interplay of masculine and feminine energies, which exist within all individuals, regardless of gender. Sherri Mitchell, a Penobscot Indian lawyer and author, also explores this concept in her book *Sacred Instructions*, describing how the feminine represents the inner world—our intuition, creativity, and connection to divine wisdom—while the masculine represents the external world, driving action, logic, and execution.

Throughout history, various traditions have described these dual forces in unique ways—Shiva and Shakti in Indian philosophy, Yin and Yang in Chinese wisdom, Chokhmah and Binah in Kabbalistic traditions, and In and Yo in Japanese culture. Despite the differences in terminology, each tradition emphasizes the same fundamental truth: these energies are opposing yet complementary, and their balance is essential for harmony and sustained success.

In leadership, the integration of masculine and feminine energies is key to fostering a holistic and adaptable leadership style. When leaders overly rely on masculine traits such as structure and decisiveness, they risk becoming rigid and disconnected from their teams. Conversely, an overemphasis on feminine qualities, like collaboration and empathy, can lead to indecisiveness and difficulty setting boundaries. Recognizing these patterns allows leaders to fine-tune their approach, blending assertiveness with EI and strategy with adaptability.

While some chakras predominantly embody masculine qualities—such as the Solar Plexus, Throat, and Crown Chakras—others, like the Root, Sacral, Heart, and Third Eye Chakras, are primarily associated with feminine attributes. Yet, within each chakra exists a blend of both energies, working in harmony to create a holistic and effective leadership approach. True leadership mastery is not about favoring one over the other; rather, it's about integrating these energies in a way that allows leaders to show up with strength, empathy, and authenticity.

Think of it as the two wings of a bird—each energy contributing to the ability to soar to new heights. Masculine energy provides direction, structure, and decisive action, ensuring that goals are met with clarity and confidence. Feminine energy, on the other hand, fosters creativity, EI, and adaptability, allowing leaders to connect deeply with their teams and navigate change with grace. When both energies are in balance, leaders can create environments that are both productive and human-centered, where strategic vision is guided by a heart-centered approach. However, when these energies fall out of balance, the consequences can ripple throughout an organization. An overemphasis on masculine energy can lead to rigid control, burnout, and a lack of connection, while an excess of feminine energy may result in indecisiveness, over-accommodation, and a lack of clear direction.

To assist in strengthening your understanding further, the following table serves as a practical guide to help you explore the masculine and feminine energies within each chakra and their influence on leadership. As you review the table, consider how integrating both aspects—assertiveness with empathy and structure with adaptability—can enhance your leadership effectiveness and create a more dynamic and responsive organizational culture.

Throughout this chapter, we have gone in depth about the dynamic interplay of the chakra system—how its states of balance, underactivity, and overactivity shape leadership effectiveness. We've shared the influence of masculine and feminine energies, understanding that true leadership lies not in choosing one over the other, but in embracing both.

As leaders, the call to balance these energies is more than an internal pursuit; it is an opportunity to redefine leadership from a place of wholeness, authenticity, and alignment. By recognizing the unique masculine and feminine aspects within each chakra, we empower ourselves to lead with strength, empathy, and purpose, creating workplaces that are not only productive but also compassionate and inspired—holistic.

The definition of holistic is characterized by the belief that the parts of something are interconnected and can be explained only by reference to the whole. It is in this collective way of thinking that we can examine the overall singular body of a corporation and how to bring holistic cohesion between all parts of it. Returning to the root of this metaphysical wisdom allows leadership to transcend putting out the symptomatic fires of corporate imbalance. As a result, CL becomes the tool for the new world of leaders healing generational wounds through the mechanism of ancient futurism.

Know that the true essence of leadership is not confined to rigid frameworks or external validation. It is about embracing the duality within and embodying the full spectrum of your energetic potential. With that, we conclude this chapter with an affirmation for you.

Chakra	Masculine Traits	Feminine Traits	Leadership Style Alignment
Root (Red)	Structure, stability, security, and discipline	Trust, grounding, adaptability, and patience	**Servant Leadership**—Creating psychological safety and trust
Sacral (Orange)	Focus, initiative, and goal orientation	Creativity, EI, and collaboration	**Emotional Intelligence**—Cultivating emotional awareness and creativity
Solar Plexus (Yellow)	Confidence, assertiveness, and decisiveness	Self-worth, empowerment, and resilience	**Transformational Leadership**—Inspiring purpose and empowerment
Heart (Green)	Strength, responsibility, and healthy boundaries	Compassion, empathy, and connection	**Servant Leadership**—Leading with heart and fostering belonging
Throat (Blue)	Clarity, decisiveness, and authority	Expression, receptivity, and openness	**Emotional Intelligence**—Transparent and authentic communication
Third Eye (Indigo)	Strategic thinking, logic, and long-term vision	Intuition, insight, and imaginative thinking	**Transformational Leadership**—Leading with vision and foresight
Crown (Violet)	Purpose, ethical leadership, and structured wisdom	Inspiration, spiritual connection, and openness	**Transformational Leadership**—Aligning actions with values and purpose

This affirmation serves as a reminder that within every leader—YOU—lies the power to balance, harmonize, and create a leadership legacy that transcends limitations. The journey ahead is about honoring both the assertive drive to build and the intuitive wisdom to guide. When you lead from a place of alignment, you unlock a higher potential—one that is resilient, innovative, and deeply human.

From this moment forward, remember and affirm:

I am Whole.
I am Balanced.
I am Masculine.
I am Feminine.
I am Aligned.

I am…

Reference

1. Motoyama, H. (1981). *Theories of the chakras: Bridge to higher consciousness*. Theosophical Publishing House.

Chapter 3

Shadow and Light
The Dual Nature of Leadership

Source: iStock/by-studio

Understanding the Shadow Side of Leadership

Leadership, at its core, is about influence, vision, and service. Yet, beneath the surface, unexamined fears, insecurities, and unbalanced energies can take hold, creating what we call the shadow side of leadership. Shadows create energetic imbalances of under- and overactive chakras and manifest as the need for control, validation, or the relentless pursuit of external success—sometimes at the expense of people, purpose, and personal well-being. In the words of Swiss psychologist Carl Jung, "until you make the unconscious conscious, it will direct your life and you will call it fate."

Jung offered profound insights into the concept of the shadow. He described the shadow as a psychological "complex"—a cluster of repressed thoughts, emotions, and behaviors that become compartmentalized within

DOI: 10.4324/9781003635918-4

the subconscious mind, often as a result of trauma, social conditioning, or self-preservation. When we encounter emotionally charged situations, the psyche, in an effort to protect itself, isolates these aspects from conscious awareness.

Jung believed that the shadow contains hidden or disowned parts of our personality—qualities we may find undesirable or incompatible with our self-image. Rather than confronting them directly, we tend to project these traits onto others, seeing in them what we struggle to accept within ourselves. In leadership, this often manifests as leaders criticizing traits in their teams that they unconsciously have within themselves—such as micromanagers who perceive their teams as lacking initiative or leaders who demand forthrightness yet struggle to be vulnerable themselves.[1]

Working in the people and HR space, Zohra witnessed a recurring struggle among leaders—decisions driven by insecurity, overcompensation, and a constant need for validation. Whether it was layoffs, relentless profit-driven focus, or transactional approaches to people, these actions weren't always about greed. More often, they reflected deeper imbalances—like a weak chakra manifesting as a need to prove its worth through external success. Zohra saw how these shadow patterns created cycles of fear and disconnection, impacting not just the leaders themselves but the entire culture of their organizations. Similarly, there's a moment that stands out to Neal during his stint in the corporate world which encapsulates the shadow side of leadership. With two and a half months until the turn of the calendar year, Neal was tasked with creating his team's budget for the year ahead. This historically involved taking the present year's revenue figures, increasing them by a baseline percentage, and reverse engineering where those revenue opportunities would come from.

Do these situations sound familiar?

Leaders and organizations may become so accustomed to the cycle of chasing higher revenue targets and increasing profit margins that they lose sight of the *why*—why they started, why they serve, and why their work matters beyond financial gain. Instead of being driven by a meaningful vision or a genuine commitment to providing value, decisions are frequently made from a place of fear, scarcity, or the pressure to meet external expectations.

In the energetic space, these unrealistic demands are fueled by imbalances in chakras, resulting in stress, burnout, and a culture where short-term wins take precedence over long-term vision and well-being. What results in the imbalances is the shadow side of leadership. It reveals itself as an obsessive focus on numbers and control, leaving little room for innovation or meaningful connection with the team. Similarly, the example of budget increases solely for the sake of greater profits, from Neal's example, shows the shadow side of leadership operating out of indoctrinated beliefs, instead of in alignment with a higher purpose (imbalanced Crown Chakra). Balancing profit with purpose requires a conscious shift—an alignment of the Root Chakra for stability and trust, the Heart Chakra for compassion and connection, and the Crown Chakra for vision and higher purpose. Leaders who integrate these energies recognize that financial success and meaningful impact are not mutually exclusive; rather, they can coexist to create sustainable, fulfilling leadership that resonates across the entire organization.

However, to truly understand the deep-seated patterns that prioritize profit over purpose, it's essential to discuss the historical context that shaped modern corporate structures. One significant turning point was the 1919 *Dodge v. Ford Motor Co.* court case that set a precedent by ruling that a corporation's primary purpose is to generate profits for its shareholders. This landmark decision laid the foundation for a profit-centric business model that has influenced corporate decision-making for over a century. It reinforced the idea that financial growth should take precedence, often at the expense of long-term sustainability, employee well-being, and broader social impact.[2]

During the late 1970s and onward, the shareholder capitalism movement in America began to take firm hold. This period of time was highlighted by a "downsize and distribute" regime marked by shareholder activism and hostile takeovers. Carl Icahn's buyout of Trans World Airlines (TWA) and KKR's leveraged buyout (LBO) of food and tobacco conglomerate RJR Nabisco are stark reminders of how immense pressure was put on companies to maximize shareholder value and prioritize profit above most other concerns which can ultimately push businesses into bankruptcy.[3] Continuing to today's time, this has fueled an energetic imbalance within organizations, where the relentless pursuit of revenue growth overshadowed the values of collaboration, ethical responsibility, and holistic success. As leaders today navigate an evolving business landscape—one where employees and consumers demand authenticity, transparency, and purpose—the need to challenge this long-held paradigm becomes increasingly apparent.

The question then becomes: how do we recognize and integrate these shadow aspects without letting them dictate our leadership style?

Interestingly, the concept of the shadow has deep parallels with Shamanic traditions, which date back more than 40,000 years, spanning indigenous cultures across the world. In Shamanism, it is believed that when a person undergoes trauma or emotional distress, parts of their soul may fragment and leave in an act of self-preservation, a phenomenon known as soul loss. These lost aspects of the self are thought to linger outside the individual, creating a sense of emptiness, disconnection, or even a feeling of being incomplete. Just as Jungian psychology speaks to the need to reintegrate the shadow, Shamanic traditions practice soul retrieval—a sacred process of bringing back the lost pieces of one's energy, reclaiming personal power, and restoring wholeness. As Shamanic healers retrieve lost soul parts, and Jungian psychology seeks to reintegrate the shadow, modern leaders must embark on their own journey of self-awareness, energy alignment, and personal growth.[4] This journey, however, is more than just professional development—it is an energetic and spiritual path. Leadership challenges such as burnout and decision fatigue can be understood as signs of energetic fragmentation. Over time, the demands of leadership can drain a person's vitality, leaving them disconnected from their core values, vision, and even their teams. In chakra terms, these experiences can result in blocked or depleted energy centers.

To prevent shadow aspects, fragmented pieces, from unconsciously influencing leadership behaviors, leaders can take proactive steps to cultivate awareness and balance. While the upcoming chapters will discuss specific chakra-based strategies, the following steps offer a foundation for self-reflection and intentional action, helping leaders to identify imbalances, align their energy, and lead with authenticity and purpose.

1 **Recognize**: Pay attention to recurring challenges, emotional triggers, and patterns of projection onto others. Journaling and honest self-reflection can help uncover hidden aspects.

2 **Reflect**: Consider how past experiences and conditioning may have contributed to current leadership behaviors. What unconscious fears or insecurities are driving decision-making?

3 **Integrate**: Engage in mindful practices such as meditation, visualization, gratitude, and chakra-balancing exercises to reclaim fragmented aspects of energy and align leadership with authenticity.

4 **Act**: Use this newfound awareness to make intentional leadership choices that reflect both strength and vulnerability, balancing action with empathy and intuition with strategy.

Leadership, when approached through the lens of energetic awareness, is not just about guiding others but about reclaiming and leading oneself first. It is about wholeness—the art of bringing together our fragmented aspects, embracing the interplay of masculine and feminine energies, and leading not just with strategy, but with heart, vision, and authenticity. Just as leadership is about embracing the whole, the shadow is an intrinsic part of that whole. Each shadow contains an opportunity for growth, for a shadow can only exist when light is present. Hidden within the shadow are strengths masked by fear, creativity stifled by self-doubt, and wisdom lying dormant beneath discomfort. Understanding the shadow side of leadership in relation to each chakra energy center allows leaders to generate self-awareness, which creates a more nurturing and optimized culture.

The path to integrating the shadow is not merely theoretical; it is deeply personal for both Zohra and Neal. Through Zohra's own Shamanic training, she experienced firsthand the profound impact of shadow integration. Leadership, for her, was not just about acquiring new skills or following strategic frameworks—it was about unlearning old patterns, facing fears, and reclaiming personal power. Immersing herself in Shamanic teachings, she identified the energetic imbalances within her leadership style and recognized how suppressed emotions and unresolved experiences acted as barriers to growth. Embracing her shadow meant acknowledging moments of self-doubt, perfectionism, and the relentless pursuit of external validation. The practices of soul retrieval and energy healing helped her reintegrate these lost fragments of herself, ultimately bringing newfound confidence and clarity to her leadership.

Similarly, Neal's journey of self-discovery and evolution unfolded through his experience in high-pressure corporate environments alongside the life-changing death of his mother. Facing relentless expectations and demands, he came to recognize how his own shadow tendencies—overworking, seeking external approval, and avoiding emotional vulnerability—were shaping his leadership style. For Neal, the journey wasn't about eliminating his masculine edge of ambition or drive, but rather learning how to balance it with the feminine aspects of presence, trust, and flow. His experiences reinforced the understanding that sustainable leadership is not solely built on strategy and execution but also on self-awareness and meeting others where they are.

Chakra Imbalances in Leadership

While recognizing and confronting the monsters in our own shadow closets is often the first step in personal growth, how does this process translate into everyday leadership in the workplace? As leaders, our decisions and actions are influenced by internal energetic patterns, whether we are consciously aware of them or not. When you begin to identify areas of energetic imbalance in your professional life, you may notice how certain behaviors—such as acting out of fear, struggling with boundaries, displaying empathy detachment, exhibiting arrogance, or avoiding speaking your truth—stem from these imbalances.

This overview highlights shadow aspects of some leadership models and their chakra imbalances, with reflection questions to guide personal growth and positive organizational change.

Transformational Leadership—Shadow Side: Over-idealism and Control

Balanced Trait: Transformational leaders inspire, empower, and motivate teams to achieve beyond expectations through a compelling vision, aligning with the Solar Plexus, Third Eye, and Crown Chakras.

Shadow Aspects:

Overactive State (Crown Chakra Imbalance):

Leaders may become overly idealistic or disconnected from practical realities, pursuing grand visions without considering operational feasibility. This can result in teams feeling overwhelmed and exhausted, as they are constantly pushed toward unattainable goals. In extreme cases, transformational leaders may develop controlling tendencies, imposing their vision without inclusivity.

Example: A leader fixated on innovation may ignore the logistical needs of the team, resulting in burnout and unrealistic expectations.

Underactive State (Solar Plexus Chakra Imbalance):

Leaders might struggle to maintain consistent motivation, becoming passive visionaries rather than active change agents. Without the confidence to drive their vision forward, they may lack follow-through, leaving their teams feeling directionless and uninspired.

Example: A leader who articulates a great vision but fails to provide actionable steps, leading to stagnation within the organization.

Reflection Questions:

- Am I balancing vision with practical execution?
- Do I empower my team to take ownership, or do I micromanage under the guise of inspiration?

Action Steps for Balance:

- Grounding practices to align vision with practical strategies.
- Establish regular check-ins to assess feasibility and team well-being.

Servant Leadership—Shadow Side: Over-sacrificing and Lack of Boundaries

Balanced Trait: Servant leaders prioritize the well-being of their teams, fostering trust, empathy, and collaboration, which aligns with the Root and Heart Chakras.

Shadow Aspects:

Overactive State (Heart Chakra Imbalance):

Leaders may overextend themselves in service to others, neglecting their own well-being and decision-making authority. This over-giving nature can lead to exhaustion and an inability to enforce boundaries, causing inefficiencies and a lack of accountability within the team.

Example: A leader who is constantly available for their team but struggles to delegate effectively, resulting in burnout and organizational confusion.

Underactive State (Root Chakra Imbalance):
Leaders might become overly passive, avoiding difficult decisions in an attempt to maintain harmony. They may struggle to assert necessary direction and structure, leading to a lack of progress and clarity within the organization.
Example: A leader who avoids conflict to preserve relationships but inadvertently creates a lack of clarity and direction within the organization.

Reflection Questions:

- Am I prioritizing my own well-being while serving others?
- How do I balance empathy with firm decision-making?

Action Steps for Balance:

- Practice setting healthy boundaries while fostering trust.
- Implement self-care routines to maintain personal well-being and energy levels.

Emotional Intelligence (EI)—Shadow Side: Emotional Overload and Detachment

Balanced Trait: Leaders with high EI cultivate self-awareness, empathy, and effective interpersonal relationships, aligning with the Sacral and Throat Chakras.

Shadow Aspects:

Overactive State (Sacral Chakra Imbalance):
Leaders may become overly empathetic and emotionally involved, blurring professional boundaries and making decisions based on emotions rather than strategic thinking. They might struggle to separate personal emotions from professional responsibilities, leading to inconsistent decision-making and emotional exhaustion.
Example: A leader who internalizes every team member's concerns, leading to emotional fatigue and difficulty making objective choices.

Underactive State (Throat Chakra Imbalance):
Leaders who underutilize EI may become emotionally detached, relying solely on logic and data to drive their decisions. This can result in a lack of connection with their teams, fostering disengagement

and low morale. In some cases, EI may also be misused to manipulate others rather than to foster genuine relationships.

Example: A leader who is overly data-driven and fails to acknowledge the emotional needs of their team, resulting in a cold, disengaged workplace culture.

Reflection Questions:

• Am I making decisions that balance logic and empathy?
• Do I set appropriate emotional boundaries in my leadership?

Action Steps for Balance:

• Practice active listening without over-identifying with others' emotions.
• Develop emotional regulation strategies to maintain focus and clarity.

Leadership is a dynamic dance between strengths and shadows. Understanding and accepting our shadow self is perhaps the most transformative part of the leadership journey. These shadows, when left unexamined, can silently dictate our decisions, behaviors, and interactions with others. Recognizing the shadow aspects of leadership isn't about self-criticism; it's an opportunity to cultivate deeper self-awareness and foster growth. To support your journey, we've created an easy-to-use table that offers an overview of how these energetic imbalances manifest in leadership behaviors. It also illustrates how different leadership styles may encounter and express their shadow aspects.

How to Use This Table:

1 **Identify Shadow Traits:**

   • Reflect on the "Shadow Self Traits" column to uncover unconscious patterns that may be influencing your leadership approach.
   • Ask yourself: *Are there recurring patterns in my leadership style that stem from fear, self-doubt, or overcompensation?*

2 **Recognize Imbalances:**

   • Assess whether your leadership tendencies align more with the underactive or overactive traits listed.
   • Consider how these imbalances may be affecting team morale, communication, and decision-making.

Chakra Name	Property	Aligned Leadership Model	Shadow Self Traits	Underactive Imbalances	Overactive Imbalances
Root Chakra	Grounding and Stability	Servant Leadership	Fear-driven decision-making, survival mode, and scarcity mindset	Insecurity, lack of trust, and indecisiveness	Micromanagement, excessive control, and resistance to change
Sacral Chakra	Creativity and Emotional Flow	Emotional Intelligence (EI)	Emotional dependency, fear of change, and suppressed creativity	Emotional stagnation and difficulty forming relationships	Over-dependence on validation and emotional volatility
Solar Plexus Chakra	Confidence and Personal Power	Transformational Leadership	Need for dominance, self-doubt, and impostor syndrome	Hesitation, low self-esteem, and lack of direction	Arrogance, over-controlling tendencies, and inflated ego
Heart Chakra	Compassion and Connection	Servant Leadership	Over-giving, resentment, and lack of self-love	Emotional detachment and difficulty forming connections	Over-involvement and inability to set boundaries
Throat Chakra	Communication and Authenticity	Emotional Intelligence (EI)	Fear of expression, suppression of truth, and miscommunication	Avoidance of difficult conversations and fear of self-expression	Dominating conversations, over-communication, and lack of listening
Third Eye Chakra	Intuition and Vision	Transformational Leadership	Self-doubt, fear of the unknown, and clouded judgment	Lack of clarity, indecisiveness, and poor intuition	Over-reliance on intuition and disconnection from reality
Crown Chakra	Purpose and Higher Insight	Transformational Leadership	Disconnection from values and spiritual bypassing	Feeling uninspired, purposelessness, and loss of direction	Over-idealism, impracticality, and detachment from reality

Transforming Shadows into Strengths

Think of shadows as a younger version of yourself—innocent, inexperienced, and yearning for attention and guidance. Fighting or ignoring our shadows only leads to further disconnection and misalignment. Instead, conscious leaders must embrace their shadows with curiosity and compassion, recognizing them as valuable teachers that can illuminate pathways to growth and transformation.

While the call to consciousness is the path to transformation and balance, the pressure to constantly perform and produce has left many leaders operating in a perpetual state of overextension. This cultural conditioning can push individuals into energetic imbalances—shadows of overcontrol, burnout, and emotional detachment that ultimately hinder leadership effectiveness. The Fair Labor Standards Act of 1938, which established the 40-hour workweek, was a monumental step in protecting workers' well-being.[5] However, today, investment bankers, lawyers, consultants, and programmers can regularly see 80-hour-plus work weeks, which have now become the norm in corporate cultures. This erosion of boundaries pushes individuals into a state of chronic stress and exhaustion. It can leave employees, especially leaders, feeling on call nearly all the time, leading to nervous system dysregulation.

Polyvagal theory, introduced by Stephen Porges in 1994, offers a scientific lens through which we can understand these states of imbalance. The vagus nerve, which connects the brainstem to vital organs, regulates our responses to stress and social engagement.[6] In a balanced state—akin to a well-aligned Root Chakra—leaders operate from a place of stability, safety, and connection. However, prolonged exposure to high-pressure environments can push them into a sympathetic state, where fight-or-flight responses take over, causing fear-driven decision-making, micromanagement, and reactivity. If this persists unchecked, individuals may enter the dorsal vagal state, characterized by disconnection, emotional numbness, and burnout—similar to an underactive Heart or Solar Plexus Chakra.

Just as the chakra system emphasizes the importance of energy balance, the polyvagal theory highlights the need to regulate our internal states and return to equilibrium. Achieving balance in leadership is not about suppressing one energy in favor of the other but rather recognizing which traits—masculine or feminine—are overpowering and adjusting accordingly. This type of growth begins with a shifting perspective—embracing the shadow with acceptance and gratitude rather than resistance or judgment. Much like dusting off an old treasure to reveal its true

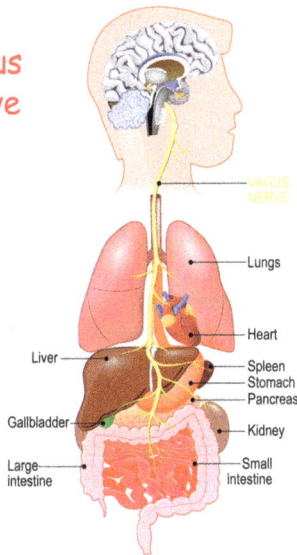

Vagus
nerve

Source: iStock.com/ttsz

worth, leaders who consciously engage with their shadow aspects uncover hidden potential and strengths that can elevate both themselves and their teams. For example, the shadow of an overconfident leader—who may exhibit arrogance or a need for control—can, when balanced, evolve into the gift of transformational leadership. Balancing leadership energy isn't just about managing action; it's about honoring the natural cycles of rest, reflection, and inspired action. Inspired action means honoring these cycles—recognizing when it's time to pause, recalibrate, and allow space for new energy to enter the system. The path to mastering leadership energy requires recognizing these rhythms and integrating practices that support both action and reflection. Whether it's through mindful pauses, delegation, or intentional moments of creative exploration, leaders can create an environment where inspired action flows effortlessly—leading to more authentic, sustainable leadership.

Recognizing the balance between action and reflection is just the first step. Real transformation occurs when leaders align their practices with their energy centers, supporting both results and renewal. The next section offers practical tools and reflection questions for each chakra to help identify imbalances and guide meaningful shifts in leadership style.

Working with Shadows: Practices by Chakra for Leadership Balance

Root Chakra (Grounding and Stability)—Addressing Fear and Insecurity

The Root Chakra governs stability, trust, and security. Its imbalance state arises from the shadow self of fear-driven decision-making, micromanagement, or resistance to change.

- **Practice:** Grounding exercises such as deep breathing, mindful walking, or visualization techniques to foster a sense of stability.
- **Reflection Question:** Where in my leadership am I reacting from a place of fear rather than trust?
- **Action Step:** Establish daily rituals that create consistency and security within your leadership.
- **Example:** Start your day with grounding exercises such as deep breathing or mindful walking (ideally with your bare feet touching the earth) to enhance stability before making critical decisions.

Sacral Chakra (Creativity and Emotional Flow)— Embracing Vulnerability

The Sacral Chakra is tied to creativity, collaboration, and emotional intelligence. Its imbalance state arises from the shadows of emotional volatility, creative stagnation, or an over-dependence on external validation.

- **Practice:** Engage in creative activities such as journaling, brainstorming sessions, or artistic expression to reconnect with emotional flow.
- **Reflection Question:** How comfortable am I with expressing emotions and allowing others to do the same?
- **Action Step:** Foster open communication within your team, encouraging emotional expression without judgment.
- **Example:** Encourage creative brainstorming sessions that provide structured guidance (masculine) while allowing free-flowing ideas (feminine).

Solar Plexus Chakra (Confidence and Personal Power)—Overcoming Control and Self-Doubt

The Solar Plexus governs self-esteem, confidence, and personal power. Imbalances can result from shadows of need for dominance, self-doubt, and imposter syndrome.

- **Practice:** Affirmations and visualization exercises to reinforce self-worth and inner confidence.
- **Reflection Question:** Am I leading from a place of empowerment or a need for control?
- **Action Step:** Delegate responsibilities and empower your team to take ownership of their roles.
- **Example:** Set clear goals to inspire action (masculine) while encouraging feedback and flexibility (feminine) to refine strategies.

Heart Chakra (Compassion and Connection)— Balancing Empathy and Boundaries

The Heart Chakra governs compassion, trust, and emotional connection. Imbalances can result from shadows of emotional detachment, over-involvement, resentment, and lack of self-love.

- **Practice:** Practice daily acts of gratitude and mindful listening to deepen connections.
- **Reflection Question:** Am I maintaining healthy boundaries while fostering connection?
- **Action Step:** Establish clear emotional boundaries to ensure a sustainable and supportive leadership style.
- **Example:** Begin team meetings by acknowledging achievements (masculine) and discussing challenges with compassion and understanding (feminine).

Throat Chakra (Communication and Authenticity)— Overcoming Fear of Expression

The Throat Chakra is associated with communication, honesty, and self-expression. Imbalances can result from shadows of fears associated with expression, suppression of truth, and miscommunication.

- **Practice:** Active listening exercises and practicing speaking your truth with intention.
- **Reflection Question:** Do I communicate openly and authentically with my team?
- **Action Step:** Foster an environment of transparency by encouraging honest dialogue.
- **Example:** Practice active listening in meetings by summarizing key points before responding, ensuring both clarity and receptivity.

Third Eye Chakra (Intuition and Vision)—Bridging Logic and Intuition

The Third Eye Chakra connects to intuition, insight, and strategic vision. Imbalances can result from shadows of self-doubt, fear of the unknown, and clouded judgment.

- **Practice:** Visualization techniques and meditation to strengthen intuitive insight.
- **Reflection Question:** Am I balancing intuitive guidance with logical decision-making?
- **Action Step:** Take time for reflective decision-making before jumping to conclusions.
- **Example:** Before making major strategic decisions, take a quiet moment to visualize potential outcomes and align them with organizational goals.

Crown Chakra (Purpose and Higher Insight)—Aligning Vision with Practicality

The Crown Chakra represents purpose, spiritual connection, and higher wisdom. Imbalances can result from the shadows of disconnecting from values and spiritual bypassing.

- **Practice:** Mindfulness meditation and connection to core values to reinforce alignment.
- **Reflection Question:** Is my leadership aligned with my core purpose and values?
- **Action Step:** Reevaluate goals to ensure they align with both practical execution and higher vision.
- **Example:** Incorporate mindfulness practices such as journaling or quiet reflection to stay connected to your leadership purpose.[7]

Leadership, at its core, is about embracing both our strengths and our vulnerabilities, understanding that within every shadow lies the potential for profound growth. By working with the energy centers of the body—balancing the masculine and feminine, the logical and intuitive, and the action-oriented and reflective—leaders create sustainable environments that foster both personal and collective well-being. The path forward requires ongoing commitment, but with each step, leaders unlock deeper levels of self-awareness and alignment, allowing them to show up with greater clarity, courage, and impact. It is within this journey that leadership evolves into a powerful force for positive, lasting change.

As you reflect on your own leadership path, remember: The ones lost are not those who have embraced their darkness, but those who have never dared to acknowledge it.

References

1. Jung, C. G. (1959). *Aion: Researches into the phenomenology of the self* (R. F. C. Hull, Trans.). Princeton University Press.
2. Dodge v. Ford Motor Co., 204 Mich. 459, 170 N.W. 668 (1919). Retrieved from https://www.casebriefs.com/blog/law/corporations/corporations-keyed-to-klein/the-nature-of-the-corporation/dodge-v-ford-motor-co/
3. Lazonick, W. (2014). Profits without prosperity. *Harvard Business Review.* Retrieved from https://hbr.org/2014/09/profits-without-prosperity
4. Harner, M. (1990). *The Way of the Shaman.* HarperOne.
5. United States Congress. (1938). *Fair Labor Standards Act of 1938, 29 U.S.C. § 201 et seq.* Retrieved from U.S. Department of Labor.
6. Porges, S. W. (2011). *The polyvagal theory: Neurophysiological foundations of emotions, attachment, communication, and self-regulation.* W. W. Norton & Company.
7. Myss, C. (1996). *Anatomy of the spirit: The seven stages of power and healing.* Harmony Books.

Chapter 4

Root Chakra

Grounding Leadership in Stability

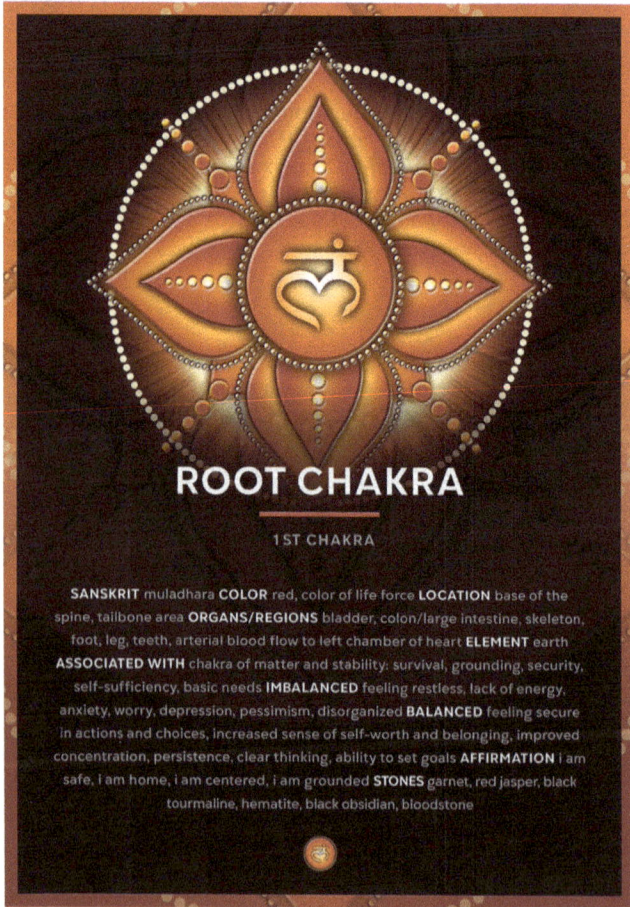

ROOT CHAKRA

1ST CHAKRA

SANSKRIT muladhara **COLOR** red, color of life force **LOCATION** base of the spine, tailbone area **ORGANS/REGIONS** bladder, colon/large intestine, skeleton, foot, leg, teeth, arterial blood flow to left chamber of heart **ELEMENT** earth **ASSOCIATED WITH** chakra of matter and stability: survival, grounding, security, self-sufficiency, basic needs **IMBALANCED** feeling restless, lack of energy, anxiety, worry, depression, pessimism, disorganized **BALANCED** feeling secure in actions and choices, increased sense of self-worth and belonging, improved concentration, persistence, clear thinking, ability to set goals **AFFIRMATION** i am safe, i am home, i am centered, i am grounded **STONES** garnet, red jasper, black tourmaline, hematite, black obsidian, bloodstone

Source: iStock.com/Nicole Marte

DOI: 10.4324/9781003635918-5

Root Chakra: The Foundation of Servant Leadership and Psychological Safety

The Root Chakra, located at the base of the spine, serves as the foundation of our energetic system. It is the source of our sense of stability, security, and connection to the physical world. The Root Chakra governs key leadership qualities such as trust, resilience, and grounded decision-making, ensuring that leaders remain steady and reliable, even in times of uncertainty.

Understanding the importance of this foundation is not a new concept. Abraham Maslow's hierarchy of needs, a widely recognized psychological framework, emphasizes that before individuals can pursue higher levels of self-actualization and self-transcendence, they must first satisfy their most fundamental needs—food, water, shelter, and clothing. Beyond these physical necessities, Maslow suggested that safety and security, followed by a sense of love and belonging, are essential building blocks for personal and professional growth. When these core needs are met, individuals can move up the hierarchy to develop confidence, creativity, and purpose.[1]

In the leadership science context, Servant Leadership closely aligns with the Root Chakra, embodying principles by prioritizing the needs of the team and ensuring their well-being. At the core of Servant Leadership lies the commitment to putting people first—supporting their growth, fostering trust, building community, and creating environments where employees feel psychologically safe. The concept of Servant Leadership was introduced by Robert K. Greenleaf in his 1970 essay, *The Servant as Leader*, where he proposed that a true leader is one who serves first, someone whom employees can relate to and trust. Greenleaf's model challenges the traditional top-down leadership approach by emphasizing that leadership is not about power or control, but rather empowering individual development and service.[2]

In CL, the Root Chakra is deeply connected to group identity, stability, financial security, and collective belief systems—those unspoken rules that determine whether someone feels included or excluded within the tribe. As a leader, your role is to provide both structure and stability (masculine traits) and trust and adaptability (feminine traits), fostering an environment that nurtures both people and processes. A leader with a balanced Root Chakra embodies Servant Leadership by:

- **Providing Stability and Trust**: Ensuring consistency in expectations, support, and decision-making.
- **Fostering Inclusion and Belonging**: Actively listening to employee concerns and creating an open, transparent workplace culture.

- **Offering a Strong Foundation:** Building systems that prioritize well-being while aligning with long-term organizational goals.

Servant leadership is often mistakenly dismissed as relevant only to non-profits. However, its core principles—people-first leadership, empathy, and the prioritization of collective well-being—are vital across all industries and organizational structures. One leader who exemplified these principles was a Chief Learning Officer Zohra worked with. His leadership style was deeply rooted in care and transparency. He regularly shared insights from books he read and even purchased copies for his team to learn alongside him. These acts of service and grounded support fostered psychological safety, enabling his team to take risks and innovate without fear of failure. On the other hand, Zohra and Neal's experiences have also brought them face to face with leaders struggling with an imbalanced Root Chakra. When the Root Chakra is imbalanced—whether due to shadows from fear-driven decision-making, operating in survival mode, or a scarcity mindset—leadership can manifest in two extremes: excessive control or a lack of foundational stability.

- **Underactive Root Chakra:** Leaders may struggle with indecision, insecurity, and inconsistency—failing to provide the stability their teams need.
- **Overactive Root Chakra:** Leaders may micromanage, resist change, and enforce rigid structures, creating an environment of fear and restriction rather than trust and innovation.

When the Root Chakra is out of balance in leadership, it creates a workplace environment where employees struggle to feel a sense of belonging. Whether it's through awkward interactions, a lack of emotional connection, or an authoritarian approach, employees pick up on the subtle signals that indicate a leader is not grounded. Over time, these negative experiences compound, leading to dissatisfaction, disengagement, and, ultimately, turnover. This disconnect is increasingly evident in today's organizations. According to a 2024 Gallup report, 51% of US employees are actively seeking new job opportunities, with only 25% recommending their organization as a great place to work. To put the 25% figure into perspective, imagine a sports team where only a quarter of the players genuinely believe in their coach's leadership and feel confident in the team's future. The remaining 75% are either uncertain, uninterested, or actively looking for another team to join. When only a fraction of employees feel a true sense of belonging and security, productivity suffers, innovation stalls, and the overall organizational culture becomes fragile and unsustainable. This statistic highlights a significant leadership challenge—an imbalance at the foundational level of the workplace.[3]

As resentful feelings build without having an opportunity to resolve one's grievances, the employees' disdain builds like a pressure cooker. Eventually, it can no longer be contained, and the worker decides that the best thing they can do is move on to a place that feels more inclusive and caring. Without a strong foundation of trust and stability, leaders will continue to struggle to retain talent and foster collaboration. When the Root Chakra is balanced, a leader's presence becomes a beacon of strength—a steady pillar that employees can rely on during times of uncertainty and a guiding force that offers clarity in times of confusion.

A practical example of creating this sense of safety is allowing employees flexibility—whether it's leaving early to pick up their children from school or attending a doctor's appointment—without attaching guilt or shame. These small acts of trust reinforce a sense of belonging and security, showing employees that their well-being is valued beyond their immediate output.

However, a lingering corporate culture of hyper-surveillance often undermines this trust. A well-known term in the corporate world is "face time"—not Apple's videoconferencing feature, but rather an unspoken expectation that an employee's physical presence in the workplace is directly correlated with their productivity. In many organizations, the amount of time an employee spends at their desk can play a critical role in securing promotions and bonuses.

With the rise of remote work, this outdated mindset has evolved into employee monitoring software, aimed at tracking productivity metrics down to mouse movements—prompting employees to use mouse jigglers to keep their screens active and avoid suspicion. This hyper-focus on physical presence rather than outcomes raises a fundamental question: where did we go astray in trusting our employees and not focusing on the quality and impact of their work?

Servant Leadership, closely aligned with a balanced Root Chakra, challenges these outdated norms by prioritizing people over processes and outcomes over physical presence. This approach moves leadership away from fear-driven hierarchies and toward environments akin to a cacao-sharing circle, where individuals feel seen, heard, and valued. The distinction lies in how employees are allowed to show up energetically within the space. In traditional, fear-based leadership structures, the organizational culture is often ruled by a top-down hierarchy, where leaders replicate the same patterns of control and pressure they once experienced from their superiors. This perpetuates cycles of "paying your dues" and disempowerment. In contrast, a CL approach—rooted in Servant Leadership principles—emphasizes a "whole-archy," where teams operate in a self-organizing, flat structure governed by a unified set of values and mutual respect.

Light Side: Stability and Security in Leadership

Throughout history, archetypes of steadfast, supportive leadership have been embodied by various mythological figures, illustrating the timeless wisdom of a strong foundation. Leaders can draw inspiration from:

- **Geb (Egyptian Mythology):** The god of the earth, representing groundedness and support, reminds leaders that stability and patience create a fertile ground for success. Leaders who embody Geb's qualities provide unwavering support and resilience, ensuring their teams remain grounded and steady, even in challenging times.
- **Ganesha (Hindu Tradition):** Known as the remover of obstacles, Ganesha symbolizes stability, wisdom, and the ability to guide others through challenges with calm confidence. Leaders who channel Ganesha's energy help their teams navigate uncertainty, providing clarity and stability without losing sight of long-term goals.
- **Zeus (Greek Mythology):** The king of the gods embodies leadership through authority, protection, and benevolence. Leaders who reflect Zeus' energy command respect while nurturing a culture of stability and structured growth, ensuring their teams feel secure and guided with strength and wisdom. Zeus Energy, as defined by Robert Bly in his book *Iron John*, "encompasses intelligence, robust health, compassionate decisiveness, good will, and generous leadership."[4]

The balanced Root Chakra in a CL naturally fosters psychological safety by establishing a culture of trust, openness, and mutual respect. Psychological safety, a concept extensively researched by American scholar Amy Edmondson, highlights the importance of creating workplaces where employees feel comfortable taking risks, sharing ideas, and voicing concerns without fear of embarrassment or retribution.[5] Leaders who actively listen, demonstrate empathy, and prioritize the well-being of their teams create a sense of security that allows individuals to bring their authentic selves to work. They create an environment where employees feel supported and valued, fostering a culture of inclusion where every voice matters—from intern to managing director. This psychological safety—rooted in the stability of the Root Chakra—becomes the foundation for sustained strength and collaboration.

A leader grounded in Root Chakra energy provides a sense of security, structure, and unwavering support, enabling their teams to thrive in an atmosphere of trust and stability. Achieving this balance requires the seamless integration of both masculine and feminine energies, as discussed in Chapter 3—each offering critical contributions to leadership effectiveness. The masculine energy brings structure, discipline, and focus, while the feminine energy nurtures trust, adaptability, and patience.

While cultivating a balanced Root Chakra is the ideal state for effective leadership, the journey doesn't end there. Achieving stability and security is only part of the equation—leaders must also confront the shadow aspects that can arise when imbalance creeps in. Whether it manifests as excessive control, fear-driven decision-making, or an inability to provide a stable foundation for their teams, these shadow traits can silently undermine leadership effectiveness. Recognizing the shadow aspects of the Root Chakra allows leaders to uncover hidden fears and limiting beliefs that may be influencing their leadership style.

Shadow Side: Fear, Rigidity, and Insecurity in Decision-Making

The shadow side of the Root Chakra often presents itself through the persistent feeling of "I am not enough." This feeling is deeply tied to our sociogenic traits the cultural and social conditioning we inherit from the communities, countries, and societies we grow up in. These traits shape our sense of belonging and survival, anchoring us in the accepted "in-group." When this foundation is shaken or there is a perceived loss of control, individuals may begin to overcompensate, leading to behaviors rooted in people-pleasing, desperation, scarcity, and fear-driven decision-making. When leaders feel disconnected from their teams, organizations, or even their personal sense of purpose, a natural sense of instability arises. This insecurity can lead to overcompensation, fostering behaviors driven by fear-based decision-making.

One of the most overlooked yet crucial skills in leadership today is emotional inclusivity—the ability to create spaces where employees feel valued, seen, and supported. Despite working in esteemed organizations, employees often cite dissatisfaction with leadership and corporate culture as a key concern. This disconnect reveals a critical failure in fostering a sense of belonging and psychological safety, both essential components of a balanced Root Chakra.

On a broader scale, history has shown how collective Root Chakra imbalances can manifest in society. For instance, during the Great Depression (1929–early 1940s), financial uncertainty crippled the economy, leading to widespread insecurity and a survival-based mentality. Soon after, the polio epidemic swept through the United States, metaphorically reflecting the nation's weakened root energy—affecting the legs and nervous system, areas associated with stability and grounding.

Similarly, at an individual level, early life experiences such as abandonment, rejection, or instability can lead to long-standing energetic stagnation, manifesting in adulthood as an inability to provide security and stability in leadership roles. Leaders who have not addressed these personal shadows may project them onto their teams, leading to environments that stifle growth in the following ways:

- **Fear-driven leadership** stems from unresolved personal insecurities and a need for control—hallmarks of an overactive Root Chakra. Leaders who operate from this space may inadvertently create a culture where employees feel constantly scrutinized and unable to contribute authentically.
- **Instability and inconsistency** reflect an underactive Root Chakra, where a leader's inability to provide clear direction stems from their own internal uncertainty and unresolved fears of failure.
- **Resistance to change** is another shadow aspect, revealing an attachment to the familiar and an unwillingness to embrace uncertainty— traits often rooted in past experiences of instability or failure.
- **Disconnection from team needs** highlights a lack of emotional inclusivity, where leaders may struggle to see beyond their own survival instincts, failing to foster a culture of trust and support.

Without a strong foundation of trust, organizations struggle to retain talent, foster collaboration, and achieve sustainable growth. Leaders who are reactive rather than proactive, or avoid difficult conversations, further perpetuate these feelings of instability within their teams.

Today, many corporations fail to honor a harmonic connection between their work and the world around them, leading to a fundamental disconnection from a grounded Root Chakra at both the organizational and leadership levels. Organizations as a whole often neglect the importance of grounding their business practices in intention and connection. However, there is a growing movement of conscious businesses that are reversing this trend by fostering a connection with their mission and values. A powerful example of this approach can be seen in a 55-acre retreat center in Costa Rica, where the founders enlisted indigenous Shamans and global healers to perform a land blessing and energetic space clearing before breaking ground on the project. These rituals were conducted to honor the land and set a strong energetic foundation for the community and healing work that would take place there.

Intentional leadership practices are more than symbolic gestures; they serve as the foundation for an organization's culture and values, shaping the way teams connect, perform, and thrive. Just as businesses that honor the history of the land create spaces infused with intention and purpose, leaders who consciously cultivate stability within their teams lay the groundwork for long-standing success. Clearing out stagnant or negative energy—whether in the physical workspace or in outdated organizational mindsets—allows leaders to align their teams with a shared vision.

Grounded and conscious leadership is about more than strategy; it is about creating a workplace where stability and security are not just aspirational ideals but tangible experiences. This creates a culture of trust and inclusivity—key elements that fuel organizational resilience and sustainable growth. However, achieving this level of balance requires intentional effort. Leaders must be willing to examine the deeper aspects of their leadership style—uncovering how fear, insecurity, and scarcity mindsets may unconsciously influence their decisions.

To support this process of introspection and deep self-reflection, we have developed the **Chakra Leadership Energy Meter**—a practical tool for each chakra designed to help leaders assess their energy, recognize patterns across key leadership traits, and implement personalized strategies for growth. Its effectiveness depends on your willingness to engage with it honestly, with curiosity and an open mind—embracing both strengths and areas for development without judgment. True leadership growth begins with awareness—the willingness to see yourself fully, without judgment.

Chakra Leadership Energy Meter

Rather than a rigid assessment or scoring system, the Chakra Leadership Energy Meter is designed to help leaders gauge their energy flow across different leadership dimensions—highlighting areas of balance and areas that may need recalibration. Leadership energy is never static; it shifts every day based on experiences, challenges, and personal growth. This tool is not necessarily about achieving a "perfect" balance but about cultivating deeper self-awareness and using insights to make intentional adjustments. Additionally, we are not objectifying what Not Often, Just Right, or Too Often means (i.e., frequency of occurrence)—this is for each leader to define for themselves. What feels excessive to one person may feel insufficient to another. Leadership is highly personal, and this tool is meant to foster self-reflection above all.

How the Chakra Leadership Energy Meter Works

Each chakra is assessed through four key leadership categories, each containing three reflective questions to help identify energy distribution. Your responses indicate whether your energy in each area is:

- **Not Often (Underactive)**: Lacking presence, engagement, or confidence in this aspect.
- **Just Right (Balanced)**: Operating in a healthy, adaptive range.
- **Too Often (Overactive)**: Overcompensating, controlling, or excessively focused on this aspect.

Before You Begin

- Pause and take three deep breaths—in through your nose, down into your belly, and out through your mouth.
- Reflect on your work and interactions over the past year. Have circumstances pushed you toward a certain end of the spectrum? Are past experiences, fears, or subconscious beliefs influencing your leadership style?
- Approach this exercise in each chapter going forward with curiosity and honesty, not judgment.
- Remember, this is not a one-time exercise; revisit the Energy Meter across all chakras regularly to track shifts in your leadership energy over time.
- Even if your energy is *balanced across all categories*, it does not mean the work is done. True leadership growth is an ongoing process that evolves based on life's situations. Reflect on what practices help, or what practices enhance your ability to achieve balance.
- If an imbalance appears, reflect on:
  - What patterns or situations might be influencing my responses?
  - Am I adapting my energy based on challenges, or am I reacting unconsciously?
  - What small adjustments can I make to restore balance?

Root Chakra Leadership Energy Meter

Mark your responses in the space provided for each question. Your responses will indicate your leadership energy in each category and your overall Root Chakra energy will be determined based on patterns across all four categories.

Category 1: Leadership Stability and Structure	Not Often (Underactive)	Just Right (Balanced)	Too Often (Overactive)
I provide direction and structure for my team.	☐	☐	☐
I establish routines and processes.	☐	☐	☐
I create stability for my team(s).	☐	☐	☐

Category 1 Result:

Category 2: Decision-Making and Confidence	Not Often (Underactive)	Just Right (Balanced)	Too Often (Overactive)
I feel grounded and confident in my leadership decisions.	☐	☐	☐
I trust my instincts when making leadership choices.	☐	☐	☐
I am self-assured in my decision-making, especially in high-pressure situations.	☐	☐	☐

Category 2 Result:

Category 3: Trust and Delegation	Not Often (Underactive)	Just Right (Balanced)	Too Often (Overactive)
I ask for frequent updates from my team.	☐	☐	☐
I am emotionally grounded during meetings.	☐	☐	☐
I manage all parts of my team's workflow.	☐	☐	☐

Category 3 Result:

Category 4: Adaptability and Change	Not Often (Underactive)	Just Right (Balanced)	Too Often (Overactive)
I create structural changes in my team.	☐	☐	☐

(Continued)

I resist change to proven processes.	☐	☐	☐
I reflect on my own sense of stability and groundedness.	☐	☐	☐

Category 4 Result:

Decoding Your Energy Patterns: Root Chakra Leadership

Category-Level Interpretation

- **Two or more "Not Often" (Underactive):** Your energy in that category leans toward instability, hesitation, or disengagement.
- **Two or more "Too Often" (Overactive):** Your energy may be dominant, rigid, or overly forceful in that category.
- **Two responses "Just Right" (Balanced) and one in another area:** Your energy in that category is mostly aligned but may need slight refinement.
- **All three "Just Right" (Balanced):** Your energy in that category is fully balanced, indicating strong adaptability and regulation.
- **One response in each area (Not Often, Just Right, and Too Often):** Your energy in that category fluctuates significantly, suggesting inconsistency or frequent shifts in response to external factors.

Overall Chakra Energy Interpretation

Your overall chakra energy state is determined by the distribution of your category results:

- **Three or more categories in one energetic state (Not Often, Just Right, and Too Often):** This reflects your dominant chakra energy state, showing a clear pattern in how you lead, but potential blind spots.
- **Two categories in one energetic state + two mixed:** You lean toward a dominant energy state, but your leadership energy is not entirely fixed. This flexibility can be helpful at times, but the inconsistency may create imbalance and execution challenges.
- **Two underactive + two overactive:** Your leadership energy is polarized, fluctuating between extremes. This may lead to inconsistent decision-making or internal tension. Focus on harmonizing both ends of the spectrum for stability.
- **Two underactive + two balanced:** You have stability in some areas but may struggle with confidence or assertiveness elsewhere. Strengthen engagement and presence in underactive areas.

- **Two overactive + two balanced**: Strong leadership traits but risk micromanagement or burnout. Allow more trust and flow where control feels excessive.
- **Incoherent energetic states (no clear pattern)**: Your responses are spread across all states without a clear pattern—this suggests flexibility but may indicate instability or burnout if energy constantly shifts. Signals the need for more intentional energy regulation to ensure you are not overextending yourself or reacting inconsistently to different situations.

Restoring Balance: Strategies for a Grounded and Stable Leadership Presence

The Root Chakra influences stability, resilience, and trust; however, achieving equilibrium is not about rigidly enforcing stability or suppressing emotions—it is about fostering a leadership style that integrates both structure and trust, discipline, and adaptability. The following strategies provide actionable steps to restore balance, leveraging both masculine (structure, accountability, and decisiveness) and feminine (trust, adaptability, and emotional connection) approaches to leadership.

Action Steps to Balance an Underactive Root Chakra

1 **Establish Clear Goals and Expectations (Masculine: Structure | Feminine: Trust)**:

- **Masculine Approach**: Develop a structured roadmap with clear objectives and deadlines.
- **Feminine Approach**: Communicate with transparency, ensuring team members feel supported in meeting these goals.
- **Example**: Model stability by setting clear, achievable goals and communicating them regularly. Encourage team members to align their personal growth with company objectives by facilitating open discussions about their contributions and aspirations.

2 **Strengthen Decision-Making Confidence (Masculine: Discipline | Feminine: Patience)**:

- **Masculine Approach**: Make small, assertive decisions daily to build confidence.
- **Feminine Approach**: Practice patience by allowing space for reflection and feedback before finalizing choices.
- **Example**: When facing critical decisions, engage key stakeholders to co-create solutions rather than feeling the need to dictate alone. Implement a "decision-review" process where you outline the reasoning behind key choices. Engage your team in decision-making to build confidence and create a sense of ownership over team initiatives.

3 **Develop Grounding Rituals (Masculine: Security | Feminine: Grounding):**

- **Masculine Approach:** Implement structured routines such as morning planning sessions to create consistency.
- **Feminine Approach:** Engage in grounding practices like deep breathing or nature walks to reconnect with stability.
- *Example:* Start meetings with a grounding exercise, such as deep breathing or a moment of silence, to enhance focus. As a leader, personally engage in mindfulness practices before high-pressure meetings to model calm and collected energy.

4 **Foster Team Stability (Masculine: Accountability | Feminine: Support):**

- **Masculine Approach:** Hold the team accountable for their responsibilities with clear expectations.
- **Feminine Approach:** Offer emotional support and encouragement to ensure they feel valued.
- **Example:** Recognize team members' efforts and contributions during meetings. Share both constructive feedback and praise, demonstrating a balance of accountability and support.

Action Steps to Balance an Overactive Root Chakra

1 **Practice Delegation and Trust-Building (Masculine: Structure | Feminine: Adaptability):**

- **Masculine Approach:** Set clear parameters for delegation with accountability measures in place.
- **Feminine Approach:** Trust the team's capabilities and allow flexibility in problem-solving.
- **Example:** Instead of micromanaging, assign key tasks to team members and offer strategic guidance. As a leader, model trust by letting go of unnecessary oversight while remaining available for support.

2 **Embrace Flexibility and Change (Masculine: Strategic Focus | Feminine: Openness):**

- **Masculine Approach:** Set structured review periods to assess change effectiveness.
- **Feminine Approach:** Encourage a culture of experimentation and innovation.
- **Example:** When a new technology or process is introduced, host brainstorming sessions to explore how it aligns with the team's workflow. Introduce a "lessons learned" session where the team

reflects on past challenges and explores creative ways to improve processes. Lead by demonstrating a willingness to shift perspectives and embrace new methods.

3 **Encourage Psychological Safety (Masculine: Accountability | Feminine: Empathy):**

- **Masculine Approach:** Establish a safe environment where honest feedback is encouraged without fear of judgment.
- **Feminine Approach:** Actively listen to team concerns and address them with empathy.
- **Example:** Hold structured feedback sessions where team members can voice concerns without repercussions. As a leader, set the tone by sharing your own areas of growth to normalize constructive dialogue.

4 **Incorporate Relaxation Techniques (Masculine: Discipline | Feminine: Self-Care):**

- **Masculine Approach:** Schedule regular breaks and enforce work–life balance policies.
- **Feminine Approach:** Promote wellness practices such as meditation and mindfulness.
- **Example:** Model work–life balance by visibly prioritizing well-being, such as taking breaks or encouraging flexible work schedules. Lead by example to cultivate a culture of sustainability and long-term leadership effectiveness.

Balancing the Root Chakra is not an overnight process; it requires patience, self-awareness, and a steadfast commitment to growth. True leadership begins with intentionality—taking the time to build a solid foundation rather than rushing through the process. By nurturing trust, fostering psychological safety, and balancing both structure and adaptability, leaders can create environments that stand the test of time.

References

1. McLeod, S. (2020). *Maslow's hierarchy of needs*. Simply Psychology. https://www.simplypsychology.org/maslow.html
2. Greenleaf, R. K. (1970). *The servant as leader*. Robert K. Greenleaf Center for Servant Leadership.
3. Gallup. (2024). *Employee retention depends on getting recognition right*. Gallup. Retrieved from https://www.gallup.com/workplace/650174/employee-retention-depends-getting-recognition-right.aspx
4. Bly, R. (1990). *Iron John: A book about men*. Addison-Wesley.
5. Edmondson, A. C. (2018). *The fearless organization: Creating psychological safety in the workplace for learning, innovation, and growth*. Wiley.

Chapter 5

Sacral Chakra

Creativity, Emotions, and Team Connection

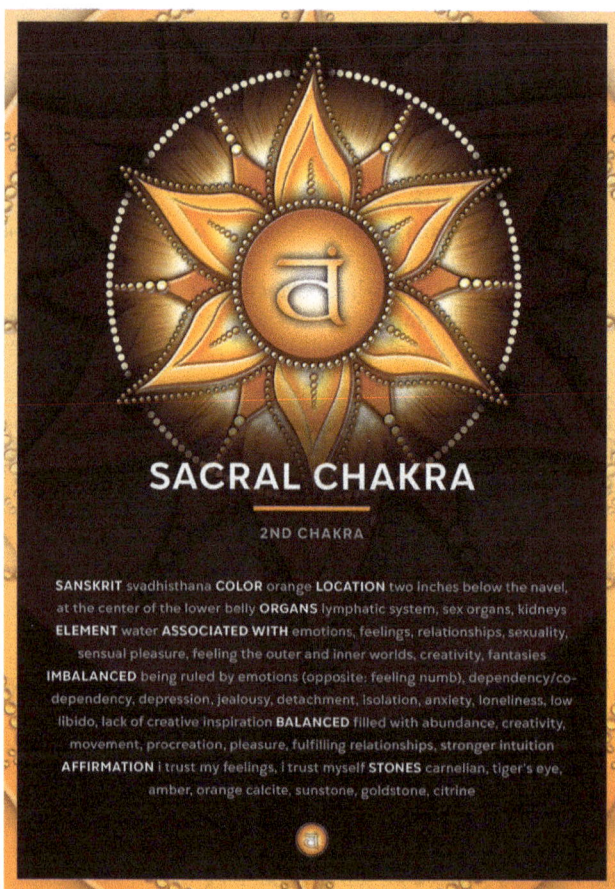

SACRAL CHAKRA

2ND CHAKRA

SANSKRIT svadhisthana COLOR orange LOCATION two inches below the navel, at the center of the lower belly ORGANS lymphatic system, sex organs, kidneys ELEMENT water ASSOCIATED WITH emotions, feelings, relationships, sexuality, sensual pleasure, feeling the outer and inner worlds, creativity, fantasies IMBALANCED being ruled by emotions (opposite: feeling numb), dependency/co-dependency, depression, jealousy, detachment, isolation, anxiety, loneliness, low libido, lack of creative inspiration BALANCED filled with abundance, creativity, movement, procreation, pleasure, fulfilling relationships, stronger intuition AFFIRMATION i trust my feelings, i trust myself STONES carnelian, tiger's eye, amber, orange calcite, sunstone, goldstone, citrine

Source: iStock/Nicole Marte

DOI: 10.4324/9781003635918-6

Emotional Intelligence in Leadership: A Sacral Chakra Perspective

The Sacral Chakra, located just below the navel, is the epicenter of our emotions, creativity, and interpersonal connections. Representing the element of water, this energy center is fluid, adaptable, and dynamic. Where the Root Chakra provides stability and security, the Sacral Chakra builds upon that foundation by introducing creativity, pleasure, and meaningful connection with others. In leadership, the Sacral Chakra represents our ability to foster meaningful relationships, embrace EI, and cultivate a culture of trust and innovation. When this energy center is imbalanced—whether through emotional suppression or overindulgence—leaders may encounter challenges such as disconnection, a lack of creativity, and toxic interpersonal dynamics.

The more self-aware a leader becomes, the better equipped they are to navigate the ever-changing circumstances of the workplace. Cultivating this awareness involves shifting from emotional reactivity to the perspective of the observer, allowing leaders to respond to challenges with wisdom rather than impulsivity. This concept of an elevated perspective aligns with the idea of the Higher Self—an omniscient, intuitive aspect of oneself that operates beyond the constraints of time and space.

According to theoretical physics models like superstring theory and M-theory, our existence extends beyond the third dimension into higher realms where past, present, and future coexist. In simpler terms, just as a two-dimensional object expands into three dimensions, human consciousness has the capacity to expand into higher dimensions of awareness. The Higher Self, functioning in this expanded awareness, has the ability to perceive the interconnectedness of our decisions and their knock-on effects across our lives.[1]

Imagine life as a vast network of possibilities. To picture this, think of a piece of graph paper, where each horizontal line represents different timelines—each shaped by the decisions we make. According to research by psychologist Eva Krockow at the University of Leicester, individuals make approximately 35,000 decisions each day.[2] Every choice, whether significant or minor, contributes to shaping our reality. Leaders who align with their Higher Self tap into a broader perspective, guiding their decisions from a place of clarity, purpose, and alignment with their highest potential.

The Sacral Chakra, intimately tied to the EI leadership model, offers a framework for cultivating self-awareness, empathy, and relationship management. Leaders with a strong connection to their Sacral Chakra—those who embrace EI—are capable of nurturing authentic relationships within their teams and with their clients. When balanced, it provides leaders with the tools needed to cultivate a thriving, emotionally aware work environment by enhancing:

- **Emotional Expression and Relatability:** Leaders with a healthy Sacral Chakra exhibit EI, allowing them to empathize with their teams, manage conflict effectively, and foster psychological safety.
- **Creativity and Innovation:** This energy fuels imaginative thinking, enabling leaders to inspire their teams to think outside the box and approach challenges with fresh perspectives.
- **Collaboration and Relationship-Building:** A balanced Sacral Chakra fosters deep, authentic connections, promoting inclusion and teamwork.
- **Pleasure and Fulfillment:** Leaders who are attuned to their Sacral Chakra find joy in their work and create an environment where their teams can experience fulfillment and engagement in their roles.

However, the shadow aspects of leadership—repressed emotions, fears, and limiting beliefs—can lead to energetic imbalances that undermine leadership effectiveness. When the Sacral Chakra is out of balance, leadership can be compromised in two distinct ways:

Underactive Sacral Chakra: Emotional Disconnection and Creative Stagnation

Leaders with an underactive Sacral Chakra often rely solely on logic and structure, ignoring the human aspects of leadership, which can lead to creative stagnation and a disengaged workforce.
Symptoms of an underactive Sacral Chakra:

- Emotional numbness and avoidance of difficult conversations.
- A reluctance to embrace creativity and innovation.
- A lack of enthusiasm and passion for the work at hand.
- **Example:** A leader who is emotionally detached may fail to recognize the personal challenges their team members face, leading to decreased morale and disengagement.

Overactive Sacral Chakra: Emotional Overload and Boundary Challenges

Leaders with an overactive Sacral Chakra often struggle with setting boundaries, leading to over-accommodation and difficulty making tough decisions.
Symptoms of an overactive Sacral Chakra:

- Emotional volatility and over-identification with challenges.
- An excessive need for validation and affirmation.
- Difficulty maintaining professionalism and clear boundaries.
- **Example**: A leader who over-identifies with their team's struggles may find it difficult to make objective decisions, leading to inefficiencies and blurred professional boundaries.

To bridge the gap between leadership effectiveness and emotional connection, leaders must recognize the profound influence emotions have on their teams. As Dale Carnegie wisely reminds us in *How to Win Friends and Influence People*, "When dealing with people, remember you are not dealing with creatures of logic, but creatures of emotion."[3] This insight highlights the essence of the Sacral Chakra's role in leadership—effective leaders acknowledge and navigate the emotional undercurrents that shape motivation, collaboration, and workplace culture. Simple yet impactful actions—such as active listening, acknowledging employee contributions, and fostering open and honest dialogue—act as modern-day expressions of honoring the creative and relational energy of the Sacral Chakra.

Light Side: Cultivating Emotional Regulation and Enhancing Creativity

A key differentiator in leadership success lies in the ability to understand and regulate emotions. People often remember how a leader made them *feel* rather than what they said or did. There have been countless instances where we've seen clients choose to go with a more expensive solution, simply because the vibe or feeling they received from the team or person offering it made them *feel* better. Emotion, being one of the oldest aspects of human consciousness, holds the key to deeper connections and influence. Leaders who develop emotional mastery—balancing their own emotional landscape while remaining attuned to others—create an environment where both creativity and collaboration thrive.

Leaders who portray the balanced energy of this chakra in communion with their Higher Self have the unique ability to trust intuitive creativity and operate from a space of playfulness, leading their teams with heightened empathy, adaptability, and strategic foresight.

At its highest expression, emotionally intelligent leadership transcends surface-level interactions, fostering genuine human connection that is both transformative and enduring. We have also seen this throughout history and mythology; leaders who mastered EI were revered for their ability to inspire and unify their people. They understood that true leadership is not about control but about resonance—aligning one's inner emotional world with external relationships to create harmonious and inspired communities. These legendary figures embodied the balanced energy of the Sacral Chakra by blending their passion and creativity with deep empathy and emotional wisdom—becoming guiding forces of change and connection.

- **Guan Yin (Chinese Mythology)**: The goddess of compassion and mercy, Guan Yin, embodies the nurturing and empathetic aspects of the Sacral Chakra. Leaders who channel her energy create environments rooted in emotional safety and deep understanding.
- **Osiris (Egyptian Mythology)**: As a symbol of renewal and creativity, Osiris represents the transformative power of EI. He teaches leaders how to embrace change, foster collaboration, and bring about creative solutions.
- **Krishna (Hindu Mythology)**: Known for his charisma and emotional depth, Krishna exemplifies the art of emotional connection and relational harmony. He reminds leaders of the power of joyful engagement, effective communication, and emotional fluidity in leadership.

Just as these figures embraced the energy of emotion, connection, and creative expression, modern leaders can channel the wisdom of the Sacral Chakra to guide their teams with purpose and passion. When a conscious leader creates the space to learn about who their employees are on a personal level—like what struggles and hobbies they have—it creates an entirely new template of connection. The employees feel more seen than they ever have before, and as a result, feel a natural and vested interest in producing top-tier output for their leader, team, and organization. On a client level, emotionally intelligent leaders can attune themselves to subtle cues—body language, tone of voice, and energy shifts—allowing them to anticipate needs and build deeper, trust-based relationships. This intuitive awareness, deeply connected to the Sacral Chakra, enables leaders to foster meaningful partnerships that go beyond mere transactions, creating withstanding, mutually beneficial outcomes.

However, one of the most significant obstacles to fostering connection and creativity in leadership is the presence of deeply ingrained money wounds. These emotional scars, stemming from financial traumas, past experiences, and inherited beliefs about money, can unconsciously shape leadership behaviors. According to Japanese author Ken Honda, individuals typically fall into one of seven distinct money personality types: the saver, spender, moneymaker, saver-splurger, gambler, worrier, and the indifferent-to-money. These archetypes, often formed in childhood, influence financial decisions throughout adulthood, subtly dictating how leaders approach risk, investment, and value creation in the workplace.[4]

When leaders are unaware of their money wounds, they may operate from a place of fear, hesitation, or excessive control, stifling their team's potential for creativity and growth. A scarcity mindset—the belief that resources, opportunities, or ideas are limited—can create a culture of competition, fear, and stagnation. Leaders operating from this space often hoard resources, resist collaboration, and inadvertently block their teams from achieving their full creative potential.

On the other hand, leaders who embrace an abundance mindset—rooted in the balanced energy of the Sacral Chakra—understand that *creativity* is the true source of value creation. They recognize that innovation, collaboration, and sustainable growth are limitless when approached with the right perspective. As Maya Angelou said, "You can't use up creativity. The more you use, the more you have." This shift in perspective—seeing abundance rather than limitations—enables leaders to transcend the traditional scarcity-driven mindset, fostering a culture where experimentation and expansion thrive.

Creativity, in this context, is not just about artistic expression; it is about bringing fresh perspectives to problem-solving. Leaders who embrace creativity naturally cultivate environments of value creation, where bespoke ideas are encouraged, risks are taken, and solutions are born from a place of inspiration rather than survivalistic preservation (underbalanced Root Chakra). When creativity is fully integrated into leadership, it becomes the driving force behind strategic initiatives, transforming obstacles into opportunities and shaping the future with intention and vision.

Beyond creativity, the Sacral Chakra teaches us that passion and pleasure are essential components of a fulfilling professional life. Work occupies a significant portion of our waking hours; if leaders and employees do not derive joy from their roles, burnout and apathy inevitably follow. Yet, in many corporate environments, the idea of pleasure is often dismissed as incompatible with productivity and professionalism. However, it is precisely when play and passion are integrated into the workplace that creativity truly flourishes. Leaders can foster this sense of joy and fulfillment by encouraging employees to align their work with their passions. Simple yet impactful initiatives—such as matching employees with projects that excite them, incorporating playfulness into brainstorming sessions, or recognizing individual contributions in a personally meaningful way—can transform the energy within an organization.

A well-balanced Sacral Chakra enables leaders to navigate relationships with EI by integrating both masculine and feminine energies—combining structure with flow, strength with sensitivity, and logic with intuition. Leaders cultivate authentic connections by fostering empathy, trust, and open communication, while setting clear boundaries and offering constructive feedback. They inspire creativity by balancing structured, goal-oriented initiatives with flexibility and emotional support for new ideas. Strong team dynamics are built through clear expectations and accountability (masculine), alongside inclusivity and emotional expression (feminine). Passion and purpose are infused into work by aligning goals with the organization's mission while encouraging employees to explore personal values. This balance fosters resilient, innovative, and connected teams.

Shadow Side: Emotional Volatility, Control, and Stifled Creativity in Leadership

The Sacral Chakra houses the energy for creativity, EI, and interpersonal relationships—qualities that, when imbalanced, can manifest as emotional volatility, over-dependence on others, or a stifling of creative potential. When leaders fail to acknowledge and address the shadows within their Sacral Chakra, they risk creating environments filled with tension, disengagement, and stagnation. One of the most common manifestations of an overactive Sacral Chakra in leadership is egoic pride—a tendency to over-identify with achievements and seek external validation. Leaders operating from this space and place may develop an inflated sense of self-worth, leading to some of the following behaviors and environments.

- **Emotional reactivity** stems from unresolved emotional wounds and a lack of self-regulation—hallmarks of an overactive Sacral Chakra. Leaders who operate from this space may inadvertently create a volatile work environment, where teams feel destabilized and uncertain about how to approach challenges without triggering emotional outbursts. Employees may become hesitant to share ideas or feedback, fearing unpredictable emotional responses. This can lead to a culture of suppression and disengagement, where innovation is stifled and psychological safety is compromised.
- **Suppressed creativity** is a common shadow aspect of an underactive Sacral Chakra, where a leader's fear of vulnerability stifles innovation and expression. Leaders in this state may stick to rigid processes and conventional methods, creating a stagnant environment that lacks inspiration and adaptability. This environment limits growth and adaptability, making it difficult for the organization to stay competitive and innovative. A lack of openness to new ideas can lead to a stagnant workplace where employees feel unfulfilled and undervalued.
- **Avoidance or escalation of conflict** reflects a leader's inability to navigate emotional complexities within their team. Whether avoiding

difficult conversations out of fear (underactive) or overreacting emotionally (overactive), this imbalance leads to unresolved tensions and diminished trust within the organization.

- **Egoic pride and arrogance** arise from an overactive Sacral Chakra, manifesting as an excessive need to be recognized and admired. Leaders operating from this shadow may struggle to acknowledge the contributions of others, often seeking personal validation rather than fostering a collaborative and inclusive environment. Employees may feel undervalued and unmotivated, leading to disengagement and a lack of commitment to organizational goals.

- **Emotional disconnection** stems from an underactive Sacral Chakra, where leaders suppress emotions in favor of logic and control. This leads to a lack of empathy and genuine connection with their teams, resulting in disengagement, low morale, and a culture where employees feel undervalued. Employees may struggle to feel heard and supported, which can result in decreased morale and increased turnover. A lack of EI in leadership can also hinder effective team collaboration and problem-solving.

- **Inconsistent boundaries** highlight the challenge of balancing emotional investment with professional detachment. Leaders with an imbalanced Sacral Chakra may struggle to set clear boundaries, either over-involving themselves in their team's personal matters or becoming overly distant and unavailable. Over-involvement can lead to micromanagement and dependency, while excessive detachment can result in feelings of neglect and lack of guidance for employees.

- **Fear of failure and risk aversion** often accompany an underactive Sacral Chakra, leading to indecisiveness and an inability to take creative risks. Leaders operating from this space may reject new ideas or initiatives, fearing the uncertainty that comes with stepping outside their comfort zone. Employees may become risk-averse themselves, leading to a culture of complacency and missed opportunities. Without the freedom to explore new ideas, teams may struggle to adapt to changing market demands.

Addressing Sacral Chakra imbalances is crucial for creating a workplace that fosters creativity, EI, and balanced leadership. Leaders who practice self-awareness and personal healing can transform their challenges into opportunities for growth and empowerment. However, leaders trapped in their shadow side may become overly controlling, driven by a deep-seated fear of losing credibility or influence. Highly ambitious leaders may find it difficult to release behaviors that once served them well, such as perfectionism and emotional detachment. These patterns, developed through past experiences—such as growing up in challenging environments—might have been essential for survival but could now hinder professional growth.

If you recognize these tendencies in yourself or others, it is time to reflect and ask: "Are these beliefs still serving me?" Just like technology that requires regular updates, our belief systems must evolve to stay effective. The encouraging news is that while changing deeply ingrained beliefs takes time, small daily practices can gradually shift these patterns, leading to a more balanced and empowered leadership style.

Unchecked pride and rigidity in leadership can be likened to the Greek myth of Icarus—flying too close to the sun, driven by overconfidence, and ultimately leading to downfall. Without addressing these imbalances, pride may escalate, leading to greater emotional outbursts and strained team relationships. By embracing growth and emotional adaptability, leaders can cultivate an environment that promotes both personal and organizational success.

Recognizing these imbalances is the first step toward meaningful transformation. Through awareness and intentional action, leaders can restore equilibrium within their Sacral Chakra, cultivating a leadership style rooted in creativity, EI, and harmony.

Sacral Chakra Leadership Energy Meter

Before you begin, take a moment to pause and take three deep breaths—in through your nose, into your belly, and out through your mouth. As you answer each question, mark your responses in the space provided. Your responses will reveal your leadership energy in each category, and your overall Sacral Chakra energy will be determined by patterns across all four categories.

Category 1: Emotional Expression and Authenticity	Not Often (Underactive)	Just Right (Balanced)	Too Often (Overactive)
I express my emotions transparently.	☐	☐	☐
I let my team openly share their emotions and concerns.	☐	☐	☐
I identify with my team's emotions and challenges.	☐	☐	☐
Category 1 Result:			

(Continued)

Category 2: Creativity and Innovation	Not Often (Underactive)	Just Right (Balanced)	Too Often (Overactive)
I encourage creative problem-solving and new ideas within my team.	☐	☐	☐
I experiment with innovative approaches.	☐	☐	☐
I create an environment of creative thinking.	☐	☐	☐
Category 2 Result			

Category 3: Boundaries and Emotional Regulation	Not Often (Underactive)	Just Right (Balanced)	Too Often (Overactive)
I involve myself in my team's matters.	☐	☐	☐
I provide constructive feedback without hesitation.	☐	☐	☐
I stay connected to my emotions in high-pressure situations.	☐	☐	☐
Category 3 Result:			

Category 4: Relational Connection and Team Dynamics	Not Often (Underactive)	Just Right (Balanced)	Too Often (Overactive)
I build relationships with my team beyond just work-related interactions.	☐	☐	☐
I demonstrate empathy in all my interactions.	☐	☐	☐
I consider my team's opinions and perspectives of me.	☐	☐	☐
Category 4 Result:			

Decoding Your Energy Patterns: Sacral Chakra Leadership

Category-Level Interpretation

- **Two or more "Not Often" (Underactive)**: Hesitation in emotional expression, creative stagnation, or difficulty forming connections.
- **Two or more "Too Often" (Overactive)**: Emotional intensity, lack of boundaries, or impulsive decision-making.
- **Two "Just Right" + one other**: Mostly aligned but may need refinement.
- **All three "Just Right"**: Strong adaptability and EI.
- **One response in each**: Fluctuating energy, signaling inconsistency in regulation or creative confidence.

Overall Sacral Chakra Energy Interpretation

- **Three or more categories in one state**: Strong tendency toward that energy, revealing both strengths and blind spots.
- **Two categories in one state + two mixed**: Dominant pattern with occasional instability in emotions or decision-making.
- **Two underactive + two overactive**: Energy swings between suppression and over-intensity, requiring balance.
- **Two underactive + two balanced**: Stability in some areas, but difficulty with emotional engagement or creativity.
- **Two overactive + two balanced**: Strong leadership traits but risks overextension or weak boundaries.
- **Incoherent energetic states (no clear pattern)**: Highly adaptable, but frequent shifts may signal instability or burnout.

Restoring Balance: Strategies for Cultivating Emotional Intelligence and Creativity

Restoring balance in the Sacral Chakra requires harmonizing structure with fluidity, ensuring that leaders embrace emotional expression while maintaining resilience, and encouraging creativity while upholding strategic direction. The key is not to suppress emotions or overindulge in them, but rather to cultivate a leadership approach that values both intuition and discipline.

We will share targeted action steps for leaders who need to activate their creative and emotional potential, as well as strategies to ground and regulate excessive emotional energy for those experiencing overactivity.

Action Steps to Balance an Underactive Sacral Chakra

*Encourage Creative Exploration (*Masculine: Initiative |
Feminine: Expression)

- **Masculine Approach:** Initiate brainstorming sessions where all team members contribute ideas freely.
- **Feminine Approach:** Engage in creative exercises such as storytelling, design thinking, or artistic expression to enhance innovation.
- **Example:** Model creativity by actively participating in brainstorming and creative exercises. Set the tone by sharing your own innovative ideas and encouraging your team to think outside the box. Introduce "Creative Fridays" where employees explore non-traditional solutions to workplace challenges, while also committing to personal creative activities such as journaling or visual mapping for strategic thinking.

*Strengthen Emotional Awareness (*Masculine: Stability |
Feminine: Emotional Connection)

- **Masculine Approach:** Set aside structured reflection time to assess emotional responses and their impact on leadership.
- **Feminine Approach:** Practice active listening and engage in deeper conversations with team members about their experiences.
- **Example:** Implement a weekly check-in where the team shares their emotional highs and lows of the week. As a leader, openly discuss your own reflections, demonstrating vulnerability and EI to foster a psychologically safe environment.

*Foster Emotional Expression (*Masculine: Assertiveness |
Feminine: Vulnerability)

- **Masculine Approach:** Practice self-expression by clearly articulating emotions and perspectives in meetings.
- **Feminine Approach:** Encourage a culture of psychological safety where emotions and feedback are openly shared.
- **Example:** Begin meetings by acknowledging a challenge or emotional experience you navigated, showing your team that emotional expression is valued in leadership. Encourage employees to share personal wins or creative breakthroughs to reinforce an open and supportive culture.

Action Steps to Balance an Overactive Sacral Chakra

Establish Clear Professional Boundaries (Masculine: Structure | Feminine: Compassion)

- **Masculine Approach**: Define and enforce boundaries in professional relationships while maintaining accountability.
- **Feminine Approach**: Communicate those boundaries with care, ensuring clarity without compromising trust and support.
- **Example**: Model balanced boundary-setting by maintaining a supportive presence without overextending emotionally. Encourage an open-door policy with scheduled hours, allowing space for support while preserving your leadership role.

Regulate Emotional Responses (Masculine: Emotional Control | Feminine: Self-Reflection)

- **Masculine Approach**: Implement structured emotional check-ins before responding to challenging situations.
- **Feminine Approach**: Engage in self-reflective practices like journaling or mindfulness to process emotions effectively.
- **Example**: Before making emotionally charged decisions, take a moment to journal your initial reaction. Encourage your team to do the same, fostering a culture of emotional regulation and intentional communication.

Encourage Team Autonomy (Masculine: Delegation | Feminine: Trust)

- **Masculine Approach**: Assign responsibilities and trust team members to execute tasks without micromanagement.
- **Feminine Approach**: Foster a culture of empowerment by encouraging employees to take ownership of their work.
- **Example**: Identify one key area where you can step back and allow a team member to lead. Publicly acknowledge their contributions and reflect on your own ability to let go of excessive control.

Leadership is not just about directing others; it is about mastering emotional adaptability and creative expression within yourself. This means going to the depths of our own emotions and learning how to be at peace with them before we can expect creativity and emotional intelligence from our teams. The more attuned you are to your own inner world, the more capable you become of unlocking the creative and emotional potential of those around you.

References

1. Bhattacharjee, D., & Roy, S. (2021). In quest of higher dimensions—Superstring theory and the Calabi-Yau manifolds. *ViXra.org*. https://vixra.org/pdf/2108.0087v1.pdf
2. Krockow, E. M. (2018, September 18). *How many decisions do we make each day?* Psychology Today. https://www.psychologytoday.com/us/blog/stretching-theory/201809/how-many-decisions-do-we-make-each-day
3. Carnegie, D. (1936). *How to win friends and influence people.* Simon & Schuster.
4. Honda, K. (2019). *Happy money: The Japanese art of making peace with your money.* Gallery Books.

Chapter 6

Solar Plexus Chakra

Confidence, Power, and Decision-Making

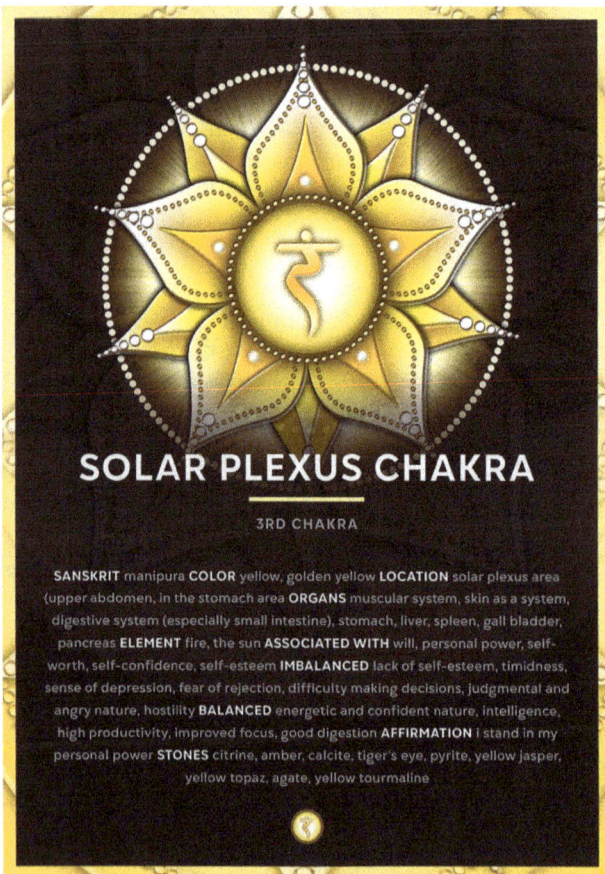

SOLAR PLEXUS CHAKRA

3RD CHAKRA

SANSKRIT manipura COLOR yellow, golden yellow LOCATION solar plexus area (upper abdomen, in the stomach area ORGANS muscular system, skin as a system, digestive system (especially small intestine), stomach, liver, spleen, gall bladder, pancreas ELEMENT fire, the sun ASSOCIATED WITH will, personal power, self-worth, self-confidence, self-esteem IMBALANCED lack of self-esteem, timidness, sense of depression, fear of rejection, difficulty making decisions, judgmental and angry nature, hostility BALANCED energetic and confident nature, intelligence, high productivity, improved focus, good digestion AFFIRMATION I stand in my personal power STONES citrine, amber, calcite, tiger's eye, pyrite, yellow jasper, yellow topaz, agate, yellow tourmaline

Source: iStock.com/Nicole Marte

DOI: 10.4324/9781003635918-7

The Solar Plexus Chakra is the energy center of personal identity, confidence, willpower, and action. Represented by the color yellow, this chakra is often referred to as the body's inner sun. It governs the balance between personal empowerment and ego. When this energy is in harmony, it exudes confidence and self-assured decision-making. It allows leaders to inspire trust and take decisive action without hesitation.

As we progress through the chakra system, we must introduce an essential concept: kundalini energy. Until now, we have focused on individual chakras, but the movement of energy between them is equally important. That movement that flows through the chakras is what we know as kundalini, fueling spiritual and personal growth. It begins in a dormant, coiled state at the base of the spine in the coccygeal center and rises upward as a person awakens to their highest potential.

When a leader consciously evolves, that is, awakens, their kundalini energy moves through the *nadis*—the energetic pathways that carry *prana* (life force) throughout the body. In Indian spiritual traditions, kundalini awakening is facilitated through *pranayama* (breath/life force control), yoga, chanting, meditation, mantras, selfless service (*seva*), and devotion to higher consciousness.[1] A kundalini activation can manifest in various ways: spontaneous physical movements during meditation, emotional clarity that drives the resolution of old conflicts, a newfound thirst for wisdom, or a magnetic shift in presence that others instinctively notice.[2]

As kundalini energy rises, it moves from the Root Chakra (foundation and security) through the Sacral Chakra (creativity and emotion), and arrives at the Solar Plexus Chakra—our core of personal empowerment. Here, energy transforms into confidence, self-worth, and the courage to take decisive action. Just as the sun radiates warmth and life to all living beings, a balanced solar plexus allows leaders to uplift and energize their teams. The sun, positioned at the perfect distance from Earth, provides the ideal conditions for growth and sustainability—not too overpowering, not too distant. This serves as a powerful metaphor for leadership: true confidence is balanced—not arrogant or overbearing, nor hesitant or fearful.

In leadership science, Transformational Leadership aligns with a balanced Solar Plexus Chakra. Developed in the 1970s and 1980s, Transformational Leadership emerged as a response to the limitations of transactional leadership, which primarily focused on performance-based rewards and rigid hierarchical structures. In contrast, Transformational Leadership prioritizes inspiration, empowerment, and meaningful change. Leaders who embrace Transformational Leadership operate from a place of authenticity and confidence which enhances motivation, engagement, and long-term commitment, making it one of the most effective and sustainable leadership styles.[3]

At its core, Transformational Leadership is guided by four key principles, known as the 4 I's:

- **Idealized Influence**: Leaders serve as role models by demonstrating high ethical standards, integrity, and reliability. They inspire trust and respect, encouraging teams to follow their lead based on character rather than authority alone. These leaders walk the talk, embodying the values they expect from their teams.
- **Inspirational Motivation**: Transformational leaders cultivate enthusiasm, optimism, and a shared vision of purpose. They communicate goals in a compelling way, helping teams see beyond routine tasks and connect their work to a larger mission. Their ability to ignite passion and drive ensures that employees remain engaged, even during challenges.
- **Intellectual Stimulation**: Creativity and innovation are hallmarks of transformational leadership. These leaders encourage their teams to think critically, challenge norms, and explore new solutions.
- **Individualized Consideration**: A conscious leader who takes the time to mentor, coach, and uplift their employees on a one-to-one level fosters a culture where confidence and leadership multiply. Employees feel acknowledged, empowered, and given space to contribute and develop.[4]

Transformational leaders inspire and motivate others through confidence, vision, and authentic presence. They foster an environment where people feel valued, energized, and committed to a shared purpose. When leaders channel balanced Solar Plexus energy, they exude:

- **Confidence without Arrogance**: Making decisive choices without the need for external validation.
- **Empowerment through Delegation**: Trusting their teams to contribute meaningfully.
- **Decisiveness and Adaptability**: Taking bold actions while remaining flexible to changing circumstances.
- **Authenticity and Trust**: Inspiring loyalty by being transparent and emotionally intelligent.

On the other side, when the shadow self is unexamined, it manifests as either underactivity or overactivity, leading to leadership imbalances. When underactive, the Solar Plexus Chakra manifests as:

- **Low Self-Confidence**: Leaders second-guess themselves and struggle to assert their ideas.
- **Fear of Failure**: Avoiding risks, leading to stagnation and missed opportunities.
- **Lack of Direction**: Appearing indecisive and unsure, causing uncertainty within the team.
- **Example**: A leader afraid of making the wrong decision frequently defers to others and avoids taking a stand. This lack of decisiveness creates confusion and erodes trust, leaving employees feeling unsupported and hesitant to take initiative.

When overactive, the Solar Plexus Chakra manifests as:

- **Over-control and Dominance**: Micromanaging and resisting team input.
- **Ego-driven Leadership**: Prioritizing personal recognition over team success.
- **Emotional Reactivity**: Displaying aggression or frustration when challenged.
- **Example**: A leader, unwilling to relinquish control, insists on approving every decision and dismisses input from team members. This overbearing leadership style stifles creativity, breeds resentment, and discourages collaboration.

Confidence-building leadership remains rare and highly sought after. According to ADP's *People at Work 2025: A Global Workforce View* survey, only 24% of employees feel confident that they have the skills needed to advance to the next job level. A leader who prioritizes self-worth, empowerment, and skill-building bridges this gap—providing what many professionals crave but seldom receive.[5]

When leaders embody the principles of Transformational Leadership, their presence in the workplace mirrors the relationship of the sun to the Earth—a powerful force that nurtures growth, confidence, and purpose. When guided by a balanced Solar Plexus Chakra, leaders create an environment where confidence flourishes, creativity thrives, and leadership is not just heard but deeply felt. A great example of this comes from Neal's early career at Goldman Sachs, where he was given an opportunity to step into his own power. As part of the company's apprenticeship culture, senior managing directors entrusted him with direct communication to Fortune 500 CEOs and CFOs—giving him the responsibility to provide market updates, pitch solutions, and take full ownership of his work. In many corporate environments, self-doubt, hesitation, and imposter syndrome are common struggles among employees. Yet, by empowering junior employees to step up and embrace challenges, these leaders exemplify the teachings of Transformational Leadership, fostering confidence, self-reliance, and delegated growth.

Light Side: Cultivating Inner-Power, Confidence, and Decisiveness

A key differentiator in leadership success lies in the ability to cultivate confidence, self-trust, and decisiveness. A leader's inner presence and energetic authority determine how they inspire and guide those around them. Teams and clients alike are drawn to leaders who exude certainty, clarity, and direction, making confidence one of the most influential leadership traits. The way leaders embody personal power and decision-making directly influences their teams and organizational culture. The energy of the Solar Plexus Chakra asks one to honor oneself through lessons which are related to the egoic personality, self-confidence, and self-esteem. Standing in your personal power means that you have clear (and respectful) boundaries as to what does and does not fly in your domain. However, leadership that stems from this chakra extends beyond external influence—it requires a profound alignment with one's sense of self-worth and personal sovereignty.

The Solar Plexus Chakra is often associated with the element of fire, symbolizing transformation, willpower, and personal mastery. In leadership, this fire represents the inner drive to act with confidence, take decisive action, and inspire others through unwavering strength. Leaders with a balanced Solar Plexus show up as a confident guide who is able to walk beside their team and show them the ropes. The light side of this energy means they are authentic as they relate to others, because most of all, they are true and honest with themselves. This sense of authenticity is what people are drawn toward like a moth to a flame. On the back of it, they are able to empower others because they know how to empower themselves. As time goes on, these leaders help their employees by providing meaningful reviews, which helps individuals foster personal growth. No, this doesn't mean sugarcoating things but rather it involves a balanced combination of both feedback and feedforward. Looking backward at past performance also creates the necessary vision and motivation by giving the tangible opportunity for practice and improvement in the weeks ahead. When these discussions celebrate current strengths and work to improve or lift up lesser capabilities is clear and actionable, the employee feels like they are an active participant in the conversation—and the energy of the light side of the Chakra Leader is in full effect within the Solar Plexus.

As previously mentioned, in leadership science this energy aligns closely with Transformational Leadership—a model in which leaders inspire, challenge, and uplift their teams. Transformational leaders' ability to cultivate trust, provide strategic direction, and encourage innovation mirrors the qualities of a well-balanced Solar Plexus Chakra. Imagine a blacksmith forging a powerful sword. The fire is essential in shaping the blade, but without control, the metal can warp or crack under pressure. Similarly, leaders must learn to utilize their power with intention, ensuring that their confidence and authority do not turn into arrogance or recklessness. True leadership is about striking a balance—using fire to create, not to destroy. Leaders who embrace this principle move through challenges with grace and certainty, knowing they have the inner resilience and adaptability to navigate any obstacle.

At its highest expression, leaders who master the energy of the Solar Plexus Chakra create organizations where confidence, courage, and inspired action flourish. Throughout history and mythology, great leaders have embodied the Solar Plexus' energy of strength, resilience, and purpose. These legendary figures did not seek power for control's sake—rather, they wielded their confidence as a force for empowerment, justice, and visionary leadership. Some examples are:

- **Apollo (Greek Mythology)**: The god of light, truth, and leadership, Apollo represents the radiance of clear vision and unshakable confidence. Leaders who channel their energy lead with wisdom and clarity, illuminating the way for others with decisive and purposeful action.
- **Sekhmet (Egyptian Mythology)**: The lion-headed goddess of power and protection, Sekhmet embodies disciplined strength and courage. She represents a leader who is fearless in facing challenges while maintaining a balance between assertiveness and wisdom.
- **Arjuna (Hindu Mythology)**: The warrior prince from the *Bhagavad Gita*, Arjuna represents leadership through inner mastery. He is guided by Krishna to overcome self-doubt and step into his duty with full confidence. His story reminds leaders that true power lies in aligning with one's purpose and making decisions from clarity, not fear.

These mythological figures illustrate the highest expression of Solar Plexus energy—where confidence is balanced with wisdom and power is used as a force for inspiration rather than dominance. When leaders step into the light side of the Solar Plexus Chakra, they create environments where self-trust, decisiveness, and empowerment flourish. Modern leaders can embody this energy by fostering workplaces where employees are trusted, encouraged to step into their own confidence, and supported in personal and professional growth.

Think of your own professional timeline. If you have been in your field of expertise (or even the same company) for 5 years, 10 years, 20 years, or longer, think back to how you felt on day three of your job. You likely didn't know how to navigate the company's systems, let alone understand the unspoken rules of leadership. Those early days were marked by uncertainty—your Solar Plexus energy may have been under-balanced, causing hesitation, or overbalanced, and pushing you to over-compensate by seeking approval. Over time, as experience and self-awareness grow, so does a leader's inner fire. What once felt over-whelming becomes second nature, and decisions that once required deliberation now flow with confidence.

Shadow Side: Arrogance, Insecurity, and the Leadership Trap of Control versus Indecision

The Solar Plexus Chakra when misaligned can result in either overbear-ing control or debilitating self-doubt. Leaders operating from an imbal-anced Solar Plexus Chakra may lead to behaviors and environments such as:

- **Overconfidence and Arrogance**: Manifests as a need to dominate conversations, dismiss feedback, and exert control over every deci-sion. Leaders who operate from this space may reject differing per-spectives, seeing them as challenges to their authority rather than opportunities for growth. Instead of fostering collaboration, these leaders prioritize personal recognition, resulting in a culture of fear and compliance rather than innovation. Over time, this stifles creativ-ity and can lead to high employee turnover as individuals seek more empowering workplaces.
- **Fear of Failure and Indecisiveness**: Leaders struggling with this imbal-ance may second-guess their choices, delay important initiatives, and avoid taking risks. Their teams, in turn, begin to lack direction and confidence in leadership, mirroring the leader's hesitation. Without a strong guiding force, employees may become risk-averse, opting for safe, predictable solutions rather than innovative, growth-oriented approaches. This creates a culture of stagnation, where opportunities for transformation and progress are lost.
- **Micromanagement and Control**: Leaders who struggle with this aspect of the Solar Plexus Chakra may believe that no one else can meet their high standards, leading them to oversee every detail, over-ride team decisions, and restrict autonomy. As a result, employees feel disempowered and disengaged, hesitant to take ownership of their work. In extreme cases, employees may become entirely depen-dent on leadership approval, stifling their ability to think indepen-dently or take initiative.

- **Emotional Instability Under Pressure:** Emotional instability under pressure is a hallmark of imbalanced Solar Plexus energy, where leaders struggle to regulate their reactions in high-stakes situations. Whether manifesting as frustration, irritability, or defensiveness, this instability creates a volatile and unpredictable workplace. Employees may feel on edge, uncertain of how their leader will respond to challenges, leading to a breakdown in communication and trust.

Since the Solar Plexus is all about drive, motivation, and pushing forward to shine your brightest, the first archetype that often comes to mind is that of the warrior. The warrior archetype represents discipline, strength, and resilience. When a leader is disconnected from their inner warrior, they may struggle with motivation, consistency, and the ability to see projects through to completion. Past failures of product launches, bankruptcies, lost deals, and negative trending quarters can also be a cause of resulting low self-esteem and an underactive imbalance in the solar plexus.

The shadow side of the Chakra Leader that gives rise to imbalances can be one who isn't in touch with their own anger and is unable to use it as a force for good to get things accomplished. Eventually, trapped anger for an excessive duration may even lead to physical health concerns such as lower back pain or liver disease. Bitterness, resentment, failure, hatred, guilt, depression, defensiveness, frustration, stubbornness, and more can similarly contribute to the shadow side of a Chakra Leader who needs to focus on the Solar Plexus. The ongoing imbalance leads to missed opportunities, a lack of follow-through, and an environment where initiatives lose momentum before reaching success.

On the other hand, an overactive warrior energy can create leaders who push too aggressively toward their goals, dismissing rest, reflection, and the well-being of their team. The energy of incessant doing, which is rampant in our modern workplace, often results in a culture of chronic stress, both for the leader and their employees. This leads us to the infamous term, workaholism. It is one of the biggest shadows of an overactive Solar Plexus Chakra, where leaders believe that self-worth is tied to productivity and relentless achievement. These individuals tend to overextend themselves, expect the same from their teams, and disregard work–life balance. Employees in this environment may feel pressured to overwork. In extreme cases, teams may experience high turnover rates, with employees leaving due to unsustainable workloads and a lack of fulfillment. As you may have heard before, "we are human beings, not human doings."

Many high-achieving leaders cling to behaviors that once helped them succeed—such as perfectionism, excessive drive, and emotional suppression. While these traits may have been necessary for survival in previous roles or life circumstances, they can become limiting when left unchecked. Just as the sun finds balance with the moon, leaders must learn to regulate their personal power, ensuring they are neither burning too intensely nor dimming their light out of fear. When a conscious leader looks at life through the energetic lens, gratitude for life's little synchronicities and subtleties help the energy move further upward.

Recognizing these Solar Plexus imbalances is the first step toward your leadership transformation. Through consciousness and intentional action, leaders can restore equilibrium.

Solar Plexus Leadership Energy Meter

Remember to take a moment to pause and take three deep breaths—in through your nose, into your belly, and out through your mouth. As you answer each question, mark your responses in the space provided. Your responses will reveal your leadership energy in each category, and your overall Solar Plexus Chakra energy will be determined by patterns across all four categories.

Category 1: Confidence, Clarity, and Direction	Not Often (Underactive)	Just Right (Balanced)	Too Often (Overactive)
I lead with confidence and authority.	☐	☐	☐
I feel the need to make firm decisions immediately, even in complex situations.	☐	☐	☐
I set clear goals and maintain direction for myself and my team.	☐	☐	☐
Category 1 Result:			

Category 2: Leadership Presence and Influence	Not Often (Underactive)	Just Right (Balanced)	Too Often (Overactive)
I assert ideas and contributions in leadership discussions.	☐	☐	☐

(Continued)

I encourage independent thinking but provide guidance.	☐	☐	☐
I inspire and motivate my team to work hard.	☐	☐	☐

Category 2 Result:

Category 3: Inner Strength and Ego Awareness	Not Often (Underactive)	Just Right (Balanced)	Too Often (Overactive)
I am emotionally stoic under pressure.	☐	☐	☐
I handle criticism and challenges with confidence.	☐	☐	☐
I am decisive without seeking input and validation from my team.	☐	☐	☐

Category 3 Result:

Category 4: Ambition and Inner Strength	Not Often (Underactive)	Just Right (Balanced)	Too Often (Overactive)
I strive for perfectionism from myself and my team.	☐	☐	☐
I tend to choose the hardest challenges as stepping stones toward my success.	☐	☐	☐
I am focused and pursue my goals with determination.	☐	☐	☐

Category 4 Result:

Decoding Your Energy Patterns: Solar Plexus Chakra Leadership

Category-Level Interpretation

- **Two or more "Not Often" (Underactive):** Hesitation in decision-making, lack of confidence, or difficulty asserting authority.
- **Two or more "Too Often" (Overactive):** Controlling tendencies, ego-driven leadership, or excessive dominance in team dynamics.
- **Two "Just Right" + one other:** Mostly balanced but with minor fluctuations that may require refinement.
- **All three "Just Right":** Strong adaptability, confidence, and balanced leadership.
- **One response in each:** Inconsistent energy regulation, suggesting fluctuating levels of confidence, control, and assertiveness.

Overall Solar Plexus Chakra Energy Interpretation

- **Three or more categories in one state:** Strong tendency toward that energy, highlighting both strengths and potential blind spots.
- **Two categories in one state + two mixed:** Dominant pattern with some flexibility but occasional instability in confidence or leadership style.
- **Two underactive + two overactive:** Energy fluctuates between indecisiveness and over-assertion, requiring self-awareness to maintain stability.
- **Two underactive + two balanced:** Stability in some areas but challenges with self-confidence or taking initiative.
- **Two overactive + two balanced:** Strong leadership presence but risks micromanagement, burnout, or an overly forceful approach.
- **Incoherent energetic states (no clear pattern):** Highly adaptable but frequent shifts may indicate instability, inconsistent leadership, or the need for clearer self-regulation.

Restoring Balance: Personal Power and Leadership Alignment

Restoring balance in this energy center requires a conscious blend of action and self-awareness. Leaders must cultivate inner confidence while also empowering others, striking a balance between assertiveness and trust, discipline, and adaptability. The strategies below provide practical steps to realign your leadership energy, ensuring that you lead with strength, clarity, and presence.

Action Steps to Balance an Underactive Solar Plexus Chakra

Strengthen Decision-Making Confidence (Masculine: Assertiveness | Feminine: Trust in Self)

- **Masculine Approach:** Practice making small, confident decisions daily to build leadership certainty.
- **Feminine Approach:** Trust your intuition and embrace mistakes as learning opportunities.
- **Example:** Begin meetings by clearly stating your perspective before asking for team input. When facing a decision, commit to a choice without seeking excessive external validation. Encourage team members to do the same, fostering a culture of confidence and accountability.

Develop a Leadership Presence (Masculine: Structure | Feminine: Personal Empowerment)

- **Masculine Approach:** Establish a routine of self-discipline, including setting clear daily leadership goals.
- **Feminine Approach:** Incorporate self-affirmation practices to reinforce internal confidence.
- **Example:** Set a leadership mantra such as *My decisions shape positive outcomes* and repeat it before key meetings. Stand tall, maintain eye contact, and project your voice to embody the energy of leadership confidence.

Encourage Team Autonomy (Masculine: Delegation | Feminine: Trust in Others)

- **Masculine Approach:** Assign leadership roles within your team and step back from unnecessary involvement.
- **Feminine Approach:** Trust that others will rise to the occasion, allowing space for their growth.
- **Example:** Delegate a project to a team member and provide clear expectations without micromanaging. Offer support only when needed, rather than hovering over execution details.

Action Steps to Balance an Overactive Solar Plexus Chakra

Encourage Team Autonomy (Masculine: Strategic Delegation | Feminine: Trust in Others)

- **Masculine Approach:** Establish clear parameters for delegation while maintaining accountability.
- **Feminine Approach:** Allow space for collaborative decision-making and shared ownership.
- **Example:** Identify one key project or task that you can fully delegate to a team member. Avoid interfering unless guidance is genuinely needed, allowing them to develop confidence and independence.

Regulate Work–Life Balance (Masculine: Discipline | Feminine: Rest and Reflection)

- **Masculine Approach:** Implement clear work boundaries and avoid overextending work hours.
- **Feminine Approach:** Prioritize rest and recovery to maintain long-term leadership effectiveness.
- **Example:** Set a "no after-hours email" policy for yourself and your team. Set an example by leaving work on time and respecting your team's time outside of the office.

Foster Psychological Safety (Masculine: Accountability | Feminine: Empathy and Openness)

- **Masculine Approach:** Establish a feedback culture where employees can speak openly without fear.
- **Feminine Approach:** Practice active listening and encourage emotional honesty.
- **Example:** Hold monthly open forums where employees can provide feedback without repercussions. Actively listen without interrupting or immediately correcting, allowing a space for vulnerability and shared perspectives.

True confidence is not about dominance—it is about standing firmly in your personal power while empowering others to step into theirs. When you embrace your whole self—strengths, vulnerabilities, and growth areas—you naturally create space for others to do the same.

As the ancient Chinese philosopher and founder of Taoism, Lao Tzu, said, *Mastering others is strength. Mastering yourself is true power.* Great leadership begins with mastering your inner world. When you cultivate balance within, your outer world reflects it, fostering a leadership style rooted in authenticity, trust, and empowerment.

References

1. Yoga Journal. (n.d.). *Kundalini awakening: What it is and how to navigate it.* Yoga Journal. Retrieved from https://www.yogajournal.com/yoga-101/types-of-yoga/kundalini/kundalini-awakening/
2. Woollacott, M. H., Kason, Y., & Park, R. D. (2021). Investigation of the phenomenology, physiology and impact of spiritually transformative experiences – Kundalini awakening. *Explore (New York, N.Y.), 17*(6), 525–534. https://doi.org/10.1016/j.explore.2020.07.005
3. Aarons G. A. (2006). Transformational and transactional leadership: association with attitudes toward evidence-based practice. *Psychiatric Services (Washington, D.C.), 57*(8), 1162–1169. https://doi.org/10.1176/ps.2006.57.8.1162
4. Place, N. T., & Fernandez, J. (2023). *Transformational leadership: Characteristics and criticisms.* University of Florida IFAS Extension. Retrieved from https://edis.ifas.ufl.edu/publication/HR020
5. ADP Research Institute. (2025). *People at work 2025: A global workforce view.* ADP. https://www.adpresearch.com/wp-content/uploads/2025/01/PAW2025_Skills_v12.pdf

Chapter 7

Heart Chakra

Compassionate Leadership and Emotional Integrity

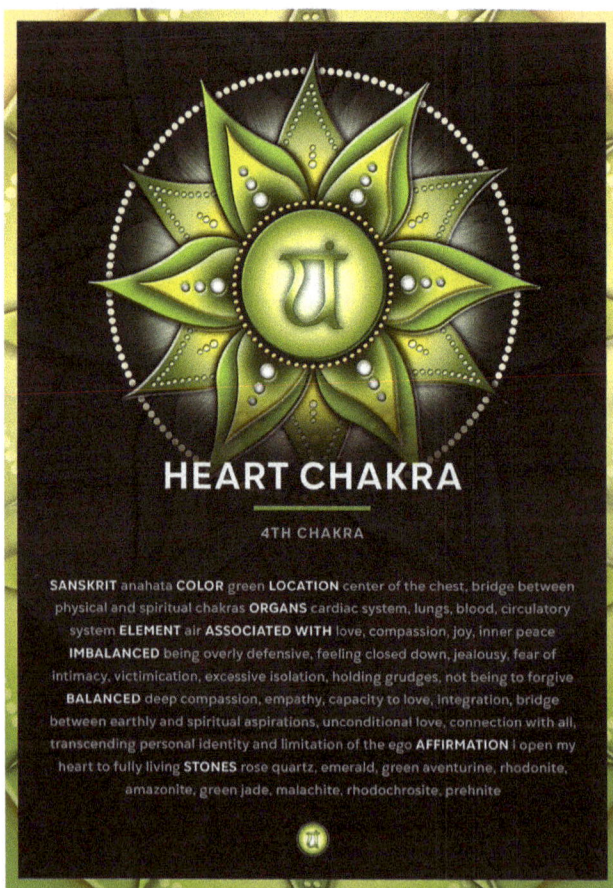

HEART CHAKRA

4TH CHAKRA

SANSKRIT anahata COLOR green LOCATION center of the chest, bridge between physical and spiritual chakras ORGANS cardiac system, lungs, blood, circulatory system ELEMENT air ASSOCIATED WITH love, compassion, joy, inner peace IMBALANCED being overly defensive, feeling closed down, jealousy, fear of intimacy, victimization, excessive isolation, holding grudges, not being to forgive BALANCED deep compassion, empathy, capacity to love, integration, bridge between earthly and spiritual aspirations, unconditional love, connection with all, transcending personal identity and limitation of the ego AFFIRMATION I open my heart to fully living STONES rose quartz, emerald, green aventurine, rhodonite, amazonite, green jade, malachite, rhodochrosite, prehnite

Source: iStock.com/Nicole Marte

DOI: 10.4324/9781003635918-8

Take a moment to pause and reflect on someone in your life who exemplifies the energy of selfless compassion and pure unconditional love. It might be a parent, sibling, partner, spiritual teacher, healer, or even a pet—someone whose presence makes you feel deeply understood and supported. Now, ask yourself: what is it about them that evokes this feeling? Is it their ability to listen without judgment, their kindness in difficult moments, or their unwavering presence when you need them most?

At its core, compassion is the ability to witness another's experience, hold space for their emotions, and take meaningful action to support them. Yet, in today's fast-paced, results-driven world, compassion often feels scarce in professional settings. Why does it flow so naturally in our personal relationships, yet become secondary in the workplace? Is it the relentless pressure to meet deadlines and the prioritization of efficiency over empathy? Or have we, in the pursuit of performance and productivity, lost sight of the fundamental truth that organizations thrive when people thrive?

This brings us to the Heart Chakra—the energetic center of love, EI, and connection. Located at the center of the chest, it serves as the bridge between the physical and spiritual realms. It connects the lower three chakras, which govern survival (Root), creativity (Sacral), and personal power (Solar Plexus), with the upper three chakras, which influence expression (Throat), intuition (Third Eye), and presence (Crown). Representing the element of air, the Heart Chakra governs relationships, empathy, and the ability to lead with love rather than control.

In leadership, the Heart Chakra embodies the principles of Servant Leadership—the philosophy that great leaders serve first, prioritizing the well-being of their teams. A leader with a balanced Heart Chakra leads with EI, authenticity, and selfless service. Servant Leaders prioritize people over profits, trust over control, and empowerment over authority, understanding that by uplifting others, they uplift the entire organization.[1]

In both spiritual traditions and leadership philosophy, the ability to lead with compassion, presence, and selflessness is considered a mark of true wisdom. Buddhist teachings emphasize compassion as a fundamental virtue. Green Tara, a revered figure representing the "Mother of all Buddhas," embodies this principle as a *bodhisattva*. A bodhisattva is a being who takes a sacred vow to help all sentient beings attain enlightenment before seeking it for themselves. This commitment is not about achieving an end goal, but about embracing selfless service as a way of life, mirroring the essence of Servant Leadership in the workplace.

A heart-centered Servant Leader, much like a bodhisattva, uplifts others, fosters emotional safety, and leads with grace. Their leadership is not driven by ego, control, or power, but by a genuine desire to serve and create an environment where both individuals and organizations thrive. The bodhisattva vow consists of four guiding principles:

- **To Save All Beings**: *Beings are numberless; I vow to save them.* (A commitment to uplifting others through guidance and support.)
- **To End Delusions**: *Delusions are inexhaustible; I vow to end them.* (A dedication to helping others transcend limiting beliefs and emotional suffering.)
- **To Master Dharma**: *Dharma gates are boundless; I vow to enter them.* (An endless pursuit of ethical wisdom and integrity in all actions.)
- **To Attain the Buddha Way**: *The Buddha Way is unattainable; I vow to attain it.* (A recognition that leadership is a continuous journey of growth, never a destination.)[2]

In Buddhist philosophy, these vows are intentionally impossible to fulfill—not to create frustration, but to shift the focus from external results to the meaning found in the act itself. This way of thinking is reflected in Zen practices, where monks approach sweeping the floor not to achieve cleanliness, but simply to be fully present in the act of sweeping. In leadership, this perspective reminds us that true impact is not measured solely by outcomes but by the care, presence, and integrity with which we show up each day. When leaders embrace Servant Leadership, they shift from chasing results to creating meaning through their actions— leading with intention rather than mere ambition. While heart-centered CL fosters connection, an imbalanced Heart Chakra can result in resentment or emotional exhaustion.

- An underactive Heart Chakra manifests as emotional distance, lack of trust, and disengagement.
- An overactive Heart Chakra can lead to overextending oneself, neglecting boundaries, or becoming emotionally enmeshed in workplace dynamics.

Leaders with an underactive Heart Chakra struggle to form meaningful emotional connections with their teams, often prioritizing logic, performance, and efficiency over human connection. While structure and discipline are necessary, a lack of emotional warmth can make employees feel undervalued and unsupported, leading to disgruntlement and high turnover.

Symptoms of an Underactive Heart Chakra in Leadership:

- Lack of emotional expression.
- Avoidance of difficult conversations, particularly those involving emotions.
- A transactional approach to leadership—viewing employees as resources rather than individuals.

- Disengagement from team struggles or personal challenges.
- **Example**: A manager who is overly focused on deadlines and metrics may unknowingly create a cold and impersonal work environment. Employees hesitate to approach them for support, leading to suppressed communication. Over time, a lack of genuine connection weakens team loyalty and motivation.

Symptoms of an Overactive Heart Chakra in Leadership:

- Difficulty saying no, leading to exhaustion and overwhelm.
- Over-identification with team struggles, taking on emotional burdens beyond their role.
- Avoiding confrontation to maintain harmony, even at the cost of leadership clarity.
- Seeking constant validation and approval, leading to inconsistency in decision-making.
- **Example**: A leader who constantly absorbs their team's stress and frustrations without setting emotional boundaries may experience exhaustion and unspoken resentment. While their intentions are rooted in care, the inability to separate personal emotions from professional leadership results in a lack of firm decision-making and difficulty addressing challenges objectively.

To restore balance, heart-centered leaders must recognize that true compassion requires both open-heartedness and firm boundaries. Servant Leadership does not mean self-sacrifice—it means leading with wisdom, presence, and sustainable care. The mindset for true servant leaders is that you are only as strong as your weakest link. When you devote time and resources to help others cultivate their weaknesses into strengths, the rising tide of efficiency due to conscious competence lifts all ships. The ability to support others without losing oneself is the hallmark of a truly empowered, heart-aligned leader. Filling your cup first and still putting others first are not contradictory—they are complementary. When leaders nurture self-love, self-awareness, and inner peace, they create boundless energy to support others from a place of wholeness rather than depletion.

What begins as a self-love journey to heal your own barriers to fully loving yourself evolves into being able to share your love with your family and friends, community, and ultimately humanity. As you shift into remembering your wholeness, you begin to see every aspect of the world around you as interconnected Oneness. From there, your priorities naturally shift. Your life is no longer lived for or focused solely on you, but rather for the benefit of everyone, as you see yourself reflected back to you in every soul and situation you encounter. In these levels of the mind, when you put others first in loving service, you are simultaneously putting yourself first through the transitive property of eternal source energy.

When we think about the heart, we instinctively think about love—and for good reason. Love has captivated the human experience for millennia. There is a reason why humans are obsessed with love. Authors, poets, musicians, and philosophers have all sought to understand love, and at its core, it remains one of the fundamental lessons of human existence. The heart is a portal that creates the landscape of a personal reality rooted in feeling. Science confirms what ancient wisdom has long known—the heart generates an electromagnetic field that influences our thoughts, emotions, and interactions.

Dr. Joe Dispenza is a world-renowned meditation researcher who has studied how the energy of the heart influences our experiences. His research suggests that when we align our thoughts (mental intention) with our emotions (heart-centered energy), we create a powerful force (activation of the quantum field) that can shape our reality. In other words, enabling us to manifest profound change in our personal and professional lives.[3]

Light Side: Embracing Compassion, Forgiveness, and Gratitude

At its highest expression, CL with a balanced Heart Chakra is about aligning mind, heart, and action—not just for personal success, but for the collective evolution of all. Where most leadership science falls short is in helping managers understand the role forgiveness and compassion play in accentuating the light side of a well-balanced leader. Everyone makes mistakes, and humans are perfectly imperfect. When disputes occur in the workplace, a wounded leader shies away from the conflict, while a strong leader who stands in their power (thank you Solar Plexus Chakra energy) shows up to confront the situation with compassion. The capacity to reconcile accountability with empathy is what ultimately strengthens trust, unity, and morale within a team.

Throughout history, great leaders across cultures and mythologies have demonstrated the power of compassion, service, and forgiveness. These divine figures embodied the essence of heart-centered leadership, using wisdom, benevolence, and fairness to guide their people.

- **Hatshepsut (Egyptian Mythology):** As one of ancient Egypt's most successful female pharaohs, Hatshepsut ruled through diplomacy rather than war, expanding trade networks and fostering prosperity. Her leadership highlights the power of compassionate governance, uniting her people under a vision of shared success rather than forceful domination.

- **Lakshmi (Hindu Mythology):** The goddess of wealth, prosperity, and well-being, Lakshmi symbolizes generosity, harmony, and nurturing energy. She teaches leaders that true abundance arises not from accumulation, but from generosity and an unwavering belief in the worth of others.
- **The Jade Emperor (Chinese Mythology):** As the supreme ruler of heaven, the Jade Emperor governs with fairness, responsibility, and moral order. He serves as a reminder that leaders must wield power with wisdom, ensuring that justice and harmony take precedence over fear and control.

These mythological figures illuminate a crucial lesson—compassion and wisdom are not signs of weakness, but rather, the foundations of lasting influence. A leader who leads from the heart cultivates trust, loyalty, and emotional resilience within their team. Just as these great figures ruled with equanimity and grace, modern leaders must learn to embrace forgiveness, most importantly, self-forgiveness, as a leadership practice, allowing themselves and others the space to evolve.

Self-forgiveness is one of the most overlooked yet transformative aspects of leadership. Many leaders hold onto mistakes, missteps, or regrets long after the world has moved on, replaying past decisions with self-imposed guilt. However, stress and regret are not rooted in events themselves—they stem from the meaning we assign to them. The mind shapes our reality by labeling experiences as good or bad, yet in their essence, situations simply are. By releasing self-judgment, leaders free themselves from the weight of unnecessary emotional burdens, allowing them to lead with centered peace. When Chakra Leaders project self-compassion, they set the tone for their teams—creating an environment where growth is prioritized over perfection and where mistakes become stepping stones rather than roadblocks.

To assist in this journey of balancing the Heart Chakras, an effective way to shift ingrained thought patterns and cultivate emotional resilience is through the use of mantras. Mantras have been used for thousands of years, dating back to India before 1,000 BCE in the middle Vedic period, as a means of spiritual discipline and mental transformation. These sacred words, tones, or phrases are believed to hold vibrational power, helping individuals transcend limitations, dissolve obstacles, and cultivate a state of inner peace.[4]

One of the most revered mantras in Buddhist tradition is dedicated to Green Tara. Her mantra *Om Tare Tuttare Ture Soha* (which translates to "I prostrate to the Liberator, Mother of all the Victorious Ones.") is believed to dissolve fear, liberate the mind from suffering, and invoke the qualities of grace, courage, and selfless service—all essential traits of a heart-centered leader. Sages who chanted mantras like these were believed to heal the body, offer protection, gain wisdom, and manifest desires.[5, 6]

Reciting this mantra for just 5 to 7 minutes daily can instill a deep sense of inner calm, enabling leaders to respond rather than react in moments of stress or conflict. Over time, mantra meditation rewires the brain, allowing leaders to cultivate EI, resilience, and unwavering presence—traits that naturally draw people toward them.

A leader with a balanced Heart Chakra is not only compassionate but also deeply grateful. From personal experience inside many multibillion-dollar corporations, we've seen that gratitude is one of the most underutilized forces in leadership. Yet, this simple micropractice has the power to transform team dynamics, enhance engagement, and foster trust. We often hear the advice to express love and appreciation to those we cherish, as we never know how long we will have with them. The same principle applies to leadership. Employees who feel acknowledged and valued are naturally more committed, engaged, and motivated to contribute their best.

In times of uncertainty, heart-centered leaders remain steady, offering emotional balance and resilience. Their ability to navigate challenges with grace and composure instills confidence in their teams, creating a stable foundation even in turbulent moments. In a world often driven by efficiency and outcomes, it is those who lead with love, gratitude, forgiveness, and compassion that create organizations which thrive—not just in business, but in the lives of the people they touch.

Shadow Side: Emotional Disconnection, Overextension, and Absence of Gratitude in Leadership

Heart-centered leadership fosters trust, connection, and empowerment, yet when the Heart Chakra is imbalanced, it can manifest as emotional detachment, resentment, or toxic workplace dynamics. Leaders who struggle to give or receive love freely—due to past experiences, cultural conditioning, or systemic workplace expectations—may unintentionally create environments that lack compassion, gratitude, and psychological safety.

This is the reality in many modern workplaces, where employees feel more like cogs in a machine than valued contributors. Millions of workers around the world aspire to a dream life that remains unfulfilled due to the detachment and dehumanization of corporate culture. Too often, gratitude and genuine human compassion feel absent from boardrooms and office spaces, replaced by an unrelenting focus on efficiency, performance metrics, and unsustainable workloads. When you ask the average person about their job, many will describe it as "what pays the bills"—a means to an end, rather than a fulfilling, purpose-driven endeavor. Employees strategically plan their paid time off, feeling like prisoners to the system, while their creativity is drained by a work environment that demands output at all costs. This lack of appreciation and emotional connection creates a disconnect between human potential and the organizations that rely on it. For businesses to evolve and meet the needs of future generations, leaders must first address the barriers preventing compassion from thriving in the workplace. This begins with examining the heart walls that block the free flow of love and connection.

Heart walls are emotional barriers built over time to protect oneself from pain, rejection, or disappointment. These walls form through lived experiences where love, appreciation, or trust were not reciprocated, causing the ego to create protective stories. Over time, these stories embed themselves as subconscious beliefs, shaping how individuals navigate relationships—including those in leadership positions.

For example, a leader who experienced repeated rejection or invalidation in childhood may internalize the belief that expressing vulnerability leads to pain. To avoid future rejection, they unconsciously adopt a detached, overly professional demeanor, suppressing emotional connection with their teams. This manifests in workplaces where leaders struggle to express appreciation, offer genuine support, or acknowledge the emotional well-being of employees. Similarly, leaders who overextend themselves emotionally—out of fear of not being enough or seeking external validation—may struggle with over-giving, poor boundaries, and eventual burnout. They may take on the emotional burdens of their teams, believing that being a leader means absorbing everyone's struggles rather than empowering others to navigate challenges independently.

Most modern corporate leaders have been conditioned into a hypermasculine workplace culture that disconnects leadership from emotion, intuition, and human connection. For decades, workplace norms have reinforced emotional suppression, prioritizing profit, productivity, and competition over collaboration, well-being, and authentic relationships. Many professionals have internalized a culture of numbing, passed down through generations of belief that one must climb the corporate ladder at all costs. The grind and hustle culture mindset—where long hours, emotional detachment, and relentless ambition are praised—has created a workforce struggling with internalized stress, perpetual exhaustion, and disillusionment.

The pendulum has swung so far toward cold, transactional leadership that the human spirit within these steel and concrete skyscrapers is reaching a breaking point. If businesses fail to restore emotional balance, yet another generation will face midlife crises, questioning whether decades of sacrifice for financial gain were worth the cost of personal fulfillment. The symptoms of this imbalance are already visible. When the Heart Chakra is misaligned in leadership, it creates environments that lack empathy and appreciation leading to a culture of silent suffering.

Common Signs of an Imbalanced Heart Chakra in Leadership:

- **Emotional Detachment:** Leaders who dismiss emotions prioritize results over connection, creating cold, transactional workplaces. This leads to disengagement, eroded trust, low morale, and high turnover.
- **Lack of Gratitude:** Failing to recognize employees' contributions fosters a culture where people feel undervalued and unmotivated. Innovation stalls, and retaining top talent becomes difficult.
- **Overextension and Burnout:** Leaders who overextend themselves trying to meet everyone's needs exhaust their energy, leading to resentment and dependency within teams, harming both clarity and productivity.
- **Fear of Vulnerability:** Suppressing emotions fosters a culture of avoidance, stifling trust and authentic communication. This weakens collaboration, innovation, and long-term loyalty.

These imbalances erode trust, creativity, and the overall sense of belonging within organizations. Yet, the solution is not an extreme shift from one end of the spectrum to another. The answer does not lie in overcorrecting toward unchecked emotionalism or dismissing the need for structure and results. Instead, it requires a recalibration—finding the balance between efficiency and empathy, between results and relationships. This is where the concept of the middle way becomes essential. The Buddha once explained this principle through the metaphor of tuning a stringed instrument. If the strings are pulled too tightly, they snap; if they are too loose, they will not produce sound. [7, 8] The same applies to leadership—if it is overly rigid and transactional, it leads to emotional disconnection and burnout. If it is too lenient and emotionally enmeshed, it lacks direction and effectiveness. Every individual leader and employee must find equilibrium within themselves. The key is harmonizing both ends of the spectrum to create workplaces where compassion and accountability coexist, ensuring leaders and teams function at their highest potential.

Leadership is not just about the external responsibilities—the reports, the meetings, and the deadlines. It is also about the internal healing, the dismantling of heart walls, and the conscious effort to lead from a place of wholeness. The micro shifts that happen at an individual level—leaders practicing forgiveness, fostering gratitude, and showing up with genuine care—create a macro-transformation in corporate ethos. This shift, when compounded, influences entire industries and even the broader collective consciousness, paving the way for a leadership model rooted in compassion, wisdom, and authentic human connection.

Heart Chakra Leadership Energy Meter

Before you begin, take a moment to pause and take three deep breaths—in through your nose, into your belly, and out through your mouth. As you answer each question, mark your responses in the space provided. Your responses will reveal your leadership energy in each category, and your overall Heart Chakra energy will be determined by patterns across all four categories.

Category 1: Emotional Connection and Trust	Not Often (Underactive)	Just Right (Balanced)	Too Often (Overactive)
I am emotionally invested in my team.	☐	☐	☐
I initiate and engage in difficult conversations involving emotions.	☐	☐	☐
I allow myself to be emotionally open.	☐	☐	☐
Category 1 Result:			

Category 2: Emotional Boundaries and Sustainable Support	Not Often (Underactive)	Just Right (Balanced)	Too Often (Overactive)
My team's needs take priority over my own.	☐	☐	☐

(Continued)

	Not Often (Underactive)	Just Right (Balanced)	Too Often (Overactive)
My team's emotional well-being is my responsibility.	☐	☐	☐
I emotionally relate to my team more than I intellectually relate.	☐	☐	☐

Category 2 Result:

Category 3: Connection and Empathy	Not Often (Underactive)	Just Right (Balanced)	Too Often (Overactive)
I try to understand my team beyond their job roles.	☐	☐	☐
I listen deeply and take others' emotions into account when making decisions.	☐	☐	☐
I focus on how my feedback is perceived, adjusting my message to be cognizant of feelings.	☐	☐	☐

Category 3 Result:

Category 4: Team Energy and Emotional Balance	Not Often (Underactive)	Just Right (Balanced)	Too Often (Overactive)
My energy is influenced by my team's emotions and interactions.	☐	☐	☐
I need to be a part of every conversation with my team.	☐	☐	☐
I invite my team to share their personal struggles with me so I can support them emotionally.	☐	☐	☐

Category 4 Result:

Decoding Your Energy Patterns: Heart Chakra Leadership

Category-Level Interpretation

- **Two or more "Not Often" (Underactive):** Difficulty expressing emotions, reluctance to address team concerns, or a transactional leadership approach.
- **Two or more "Too Often" (Overactive):** Over-identification with team struggles, difficulty setting boundaries, or prioritizing harmony over necessary leadership actions.
- **Two "Just Right" + one other:** Mostly aligned but may need refinement in emotional regulation or team connection.
- **All three "Just Right":** Strong adaptability and EI, balancing empathy with leadership clarity.
- **One response in each:** Fluctuating energy, signaling inconsistency in EI, boundaries, or team engagement.

Overall Heart Chakra Energy Interpretation

- **Three or more categories in one state:** Strong tendency toward that energy, indicating leadership patterns and potential blind spots.
- **Two categories in one state + two mixed:** A dominant emotional pattern with occasional instability in relationships or decision-making.
- **Two underactive + two overactive:** Swinging between emotional detachment and over-involvement, requiring intentional recalibration.
- **Two underactive + two balanced:** Stability in some areas but a struggle with emotional engagement, team connection, or openness.
- **Two overactive + two balanced:** Strong EI but potential overextension, difficulty maintaining boundaries, or exhaustion.
- **Incoherent energetic states (no clear pattern):** Highly adaptable, but frequent shifts in emotional engagement may signal instability, leadership fatigue, or a need for energy regulation.

Restoring Balance: Strategies for Trust and Emotional Connection

A well-balanced Heart Chakra allows leaders to create workplaces where trust, EI, and appreciation thrive. However, sustaining this balance requires continuous self-awareness, intentional practice, and emotional discipline. The following strategies offer practical steps to help restore balance, ensuring that heart-centered leadership remains empowering, sustainable, and effective across both masculine and feminine centers.

Action Steps to Balance an Underactive Heart Chakra

Cultivating Gratitude and Employee Recognition (Masculine: Acknowledgment | Feminine: Appreciation)

- **Masculine Approach:** Implement a structured recognition program where employees are publicly acknowledged for contributions.
- **Feminine Approach:** Incorporate verbal appreciation and personal check-ins to ensure employees feel seen and valued.
- **Example:** Introduce a "Recognition Ritual" at the start of meetings where leaders highlight individual contributions. Over time, this creates a culture of appreciation, increasing morale, retention, and employee engagement. Additionally, handwritten thank-you notes or personalized acknowledgments foster a deeper emotional connection within the team.

Encouraging Open Communication and Emotional Safety (Masculine: Structure | Feminine: Openness)

- **Masculine Approach:** Schedule regular feedback sessions where employees can share concerns in a structured way.
- **Feminine Approach:** Foster a culture of active listening and open dialogue, ensuring employees feel safe to express themselves.
- **Example:** Leaders who normalize open dialogue prevent workplace resentment and disengagement. Encourage an anonymous feedback channel or one-on-one emotional check-ins, reinforcing that employees' concerns and feelings are acknowledged and valued.

Practicing Vulnerability in Leadership (Masculine: Transparency | Feminine: Authenticity)

- **Masculine Approach:** Share key leadership challenges and lessons learned, demonstrating strength in transparency.
- **Feminine Approach:** Acknowledge personal struggles and growth moments, modeling emotional authenticity for employees.
- **Example:** A leader who openly admits to learning from past mistakes fosters a culture where employees feel safe to grow, innovate, and take calculated risks without fear of judgment. Sharing a personal challenge and how it was overcome builds trust and makes leadership more relatable.

Action Steps to Balance an Overactive Heart Chakra

Setting Emotional Boundaries Without Losing Compassion
(Masculine: Boundaries | Feminine: Empathy)

- **Masculine Approach**: Establish clear leadership boundaries—defining what is and isn't a leader's responsibility.
- **Feminine Approach**: Communicate these boundaries with empathy, ensuring team members feel supported, not abandoned.
- **Example**: If a team member consistently brings personal struggles into work discussions, acknowledge their feelings but redirect them toward appropriate resources, such as HR or an employee-assistance/support program(s). This ensures leaders provide emotional support without becoming an emotional crutch.

Practicing Self-Forgiveness and Self-Compassion (Masculine: Reflection | Feminine: Nurturing)

- **Masculine Approach**: Reflect on past decisions without excessive self-judgment, acknowledging that leadership is an evolving journey.
- **Feminine Approach**: Write a self-compassion letter, affirming your worth beyond what you do for others.
- **Example**: Leaders who practice self-forgiveness lead from a place of inner peace, preventing resentment and emotional exhaustion from overextending themselves. Daily affirmations or journaling reflections on leadership wins and lessons learned help leaders shift their focus from self-criticism to growth.

Fostering Team Autonomy and Avoiding Over-Functioning
(Masculine: Delegation | Feminine: Trust)

- **Masculine Approach**: Delegate leadership responsibilities and trust employees to take ownership of their roles.
- **Feminine Approach**: Resist the urge to fix every problem; instead, guide employees toward their own solutions.
- **Example**: Instead of constantly stepping in to resolve conflicts, empower employees to mediate their own disagreements, ensuring long-term problem-solving abilities.

One of the core purposes in life is to love. Especially with an open heart. The Heart Chakra is the energetic bridge between the physical and spiritual aspects of leadership, holding the immense power of balance—between giving and receiving, action and stillness, and strength and vulnerability. A leader's ability to lead with heart determines not only their success but the depth of impact they leave on the people around them.

Restoring balance in the Heart Chakra is not a one-time task—it is an ongoing practice that evolves alongside your leadership journey. Each moment of self-reflection, every instance of gratitude expressed, and each time you model vulnerability with strength, it contributes to a culture of connection. Whether we look at spiritual teachings or modern leadership theories, the message remains the same: the strongest leaders are not those who seek power, but those who empower. By embracing the lessons of the bodhisattva vow, the science of the heart's energy field, and the wisdom of Servant Leadership, we allow ourselves to lead with compassion and magnetic influence.

References

1. Greenleaf Center for Servant Leadership. (n.d.). *What is servant leadership?* Retrieved from https://www.greenleaf.org/what-is-servant-leadership/
2. Thurman, R. A. F. (1998). *Essential Tibetan Buddhism*. HarperOne.
3. Dispenza, J. (2017). *Becoming supernatural: How common people are doing the uncommon*. Hay House.
4. Flood, G. (1996). *An introduction to Hinduism*. Cambridge University Press.
5. Beer, R. (2003). *The handbook of Tibetan Buddhist symbols*. Shambhala Publications.
6. Mal, A. (2016). Mantra chanting heals and connects. *Harvard Divinity Bulletin*. Retrieved from https://bulletin.hds.harvard.edu/mantra-chanting-heals-and-connects/
7. Bodhi, B. (Trans.). (2012). *The Numerical Discourses of the Buddha: A Translation of the Aṅguttara Nikāya* (p. 909). Wisdom Publications.
8. Weinstein, T. (n.d.). *Not too tight, not too loose*. Kripalu. Retrieved from https://kripalu.org/resources/not-too-tight-not-too-loose

Chapter 8

Throat Chakra

Authentic Communication and Truth

THROAT CHAKRA

5TH CHAKRA

SANSKRIT vishuddha COLOR light blue, turquoise LOCATION base of the throat ORGANS lungs, bronchi, oesophagus/trachea, voice, throat, neck, jaw, chin, cheeks ELEMENT sound or space ASSOCIATED WITH communication, inspiration, self-expression, independence, truth IMBALANCED shyness, inhibitions, confusion, fear of isolation, not being able to listen to others, fame-seeking, manipulating, dishonesty, social anxiety BALANCED strong and clear self-expression, good communication skills (understanding, comprehension), expressing feelings, balance between feeling and thinking AFFIRMATION I am expressing myself with clear intent STONES amazonite, turquoise, aquamarine, lapis lazuli, sodalite, blue apatite, blue lace agate

Source: iStock.com/Nicole Marte

DOI: 10.4324/9781003635918-9

The Throat Chakra, located at the base of the throat, is the energy center of communication, self-expression, and truth. It governs our ability to speak with integrity and is the bridge between inner truth and external expression, allowing leaders to align their words with their values and vision. The energy moving up from the heart is what feeds the throat from the pranic perspective. When this energy is rooted in love and service, the emotional finesse that the Throat Chakra delivers the communication with is what separates a novice from an expert.

The Throat Chakra is linked to the element of sound, emphasizing the vibrational impact of our words. Whether spoken aloud or communicated through tone, pitch, and inflection, every word carries energy—influencing how people perceive and respond to leadership. When balanced, the Throat Chakra enables leaders to speak with gravitas, inspire action, and foster pragmatism. However, when misaligned, it can lead to either suppressed communication (fear of speaking up, avoidance of difficult conversations) or overcommunication (speaking without clarity, dominating discussions, or creating confusion).

From an early age, we're told, "you have two ears and one mouth for a reason—listen twice as much as you speak." While simple, this wisdom holds deep truth. Effective communication begins with active listening. Even as infants, we first learn to listen and observe before forming words, making listening the natural precursor to speech. In leadership, discernment in communication—knowing when to listen, when to speak, and how to deliver a message—is an invaluable skill that sets apart those who lead with inspiration. Ironically, those who overshare or dominate discussions often do so to cover up insecurities or internal imbalances. This is an unconscious defense mechanism—speaking excessively in an attempt to control perception or mask vulnerability. In contrast, those who struggle to express themselves may have learned early on that their voice was not valued or that speaking up led to negative consequences. Both tendencies—withholding expression or over-explaining—are signs of an imbalanced Throat Chakra. The key is to listen first, speak with intention, and communicate from a place of personal truth rather than fear.

In leadership, effective communication is inseparable from EI. A leader's voice has the power to motivate, align teams, and cultivate a culture of inclusion. Rather than simply delivering information, EI leaders create an environment where open dialogue, constructive feedback, and shared vision thrive. The distinction between ego-driven speech and truth-aligned communication is crucial for leadership. Leaders who speak from authenticity and alignment inspire confidence and trust, while those who communicate from fear or attachment to external validation can come across as inauthentic, manipulative, or reactive.

A leader's ability to communicate effectively is deeply tied to their emotional self-awareness and capacity for active listening. Emotionally intelligent leaders do not react impulsively; they take the time to understand different perspectives, regulate their emotions, and choose their words with care. They recognize that tone, timing, and delivery all impact how their message is received, ensuring that communication fosters psychological safety, openness, and mutual respect within their teams.

People naturally gravitate toward those who speak from inner authority rather than external validation. Authenticity is not just something we hear—it is something we feel. It is the unspoken energy behind a leader's words, the resonance of integrity that fosters a desire to rally behind their vision. When leaders speak their truth with transparency, conviction, and EI, their communication becomes a catalyst for transformation, driving purpose-driven action and meaningful change.

Light Side: Speaking with Truth, Clarity, and Emotional Intelligence

True leadership is not about speaking the loudest but about communicating with intention. The key to mastering Throat Chakra energy in leadership is learning to balance assertiveness with receptivity, authenticity with diplomacy, and expression with active listening. By recognizing where their communication tendencies fall on the spectrum, leaders can refine their approach, ensuring they listen as much as they speak to inspire without overwhelming.

A leader who embodies the light side (i.e., balanced state) of the Throat Chakra is a conscious communicator, navigating conversations with awareness, clarity, and EI. They speak their truth with confidence while also making space for others to express theirs. These leaders:

- Communicate with clarity and transparency, ensuring that their words unify rather than divide.
- Encourage open dialogue, fostering a work culture where employees feel psychologically safe to share ideas.
- Listen before they speak, making sure they understand before responding.
- Use EI to navigate difficult conversations with empathy and grace.

This alignment between thought, speech, and action is not just a leadership principle—it is a fundamental truth of higher consciousness. In some spiritual teachings, it is believed that as humanity evolves into a lighter density of existence, communication will transcend words and operate solely through instantaneous knowing. At these levels, all thoughts among conscious beings are transferred at the level of the mind, rooted in unconditional love and truth.[1] Deception becomes impossible because all communication flows from absolute authenticity.

While we may not yet exist in such a universally connected state, we already experience glimpses of this truth in leadership and relationships. Think of a time when you sensed someone was not being fully honest, even though their words sounded convincing. This is because communication is more than just language—it carries an underlying energy and unheard frequency. People don't just hear words; they feel them. Leaders who embody the light side of the Throat Chakra understand this at the deepest level.

For these leaders, authenticity starts in the mind before it is ever spoken aloud. They recognize that clarity in thought leads to clarity in speech, and that leadership communication should always be aligned with truth, EI, and ethical responsibility. A leader in balance does not manipulate narratives or speak from a place of insecurity—they speak with integrity, listen with intention, and act with conviction.

Thus, emotionally intelligent leadership ensures that thoughts, words, and actions remain congruent. By doing so, they display the highest expression of CL—where communication is not just about delivering a message, but about creating resonance, trust, and meaningful transformation.

This principle of truth-aligned leadership is not new. Throughout history, mythological figures have embodied the transformative power of communication and self-expression. These legendary leaders, deities, and sages illustrate the highest expression of the Throat Chakra, showing how speech, when guided by integrity and EI, can inspire nations, resolve conflicts, and shape the course of history.

- **Thoth (Egyptian Mythology):** Thoth, the Egyptian God of Writing, and speech, was regarded as the divine scribe who recorded all knowledge and maintained balance through language. He was seen as the mediator of the gods, resolving disputes and bringing clarity through his articulate and measured words. Thoth's mastery of communication and deep understanding of truth reflect the power of an aligned Throat Chakra, and leaders can learn from Thoth by valuing clear, thoughtful communication that fosters understanding, collaboration, and ethical decision-making.
- **Saraswati (Hindu Mythology):** Saraswati, the Hindu Goddess of Learning, and speech, embodies the power of creative expression and articulate thought. She is associated with eloquence, clarity of mind, and the ability to communicate higher truths with grace and

intelligence. Leaders who channel Saraswati's energy prioritize knowledge-sharing, inspire with their words, and cultivate an environment where honest and meaningful dialogue flourishes. Saraswati teaches that a leader's voice should uplift, educate, and empower others rather than create confusion or discord.

- **Odin (Norse Mythology):** Odin, the Chief Deity of Norse Mythology, was obsessed with the pursuit of knowledge—so much so that he sacrificed an eye for deeper understanding. He was also the god of poetry, language, and the mystical power of runes, using words to shape reality and influence fate. Odin's connection to language as a tool of transformation and his relentless quest for truth make him a fitting symbol of an awakened Throat Chakra. Leaders inspired by Odin embrace continuous learning, seek truth beyond surface appearances, and wield their words with precision—knowing that communication has the power to inspire or destroy.

True leadership communication is not about saying more—it is about saying what matters, with purpose, precision, and presence. A leader with a balanced Throat Chakra understands that words are not just tools for communication—they are instruments of transformation. The ability to express truth with clarity, EI, and alignment is what separates impactful leaders from those who merely manage. Just as the great mythological figures used speech as a force for wisdom and transformation, today's leaders must recognize that their words shape the cultures they lead.

Shadow Side: Miscommunication, Overcontrol, and Fear of Vulnerability in Leadership

Words are powerful—they can either build or break. To that extent, language is not just a tool for expression; it is an energetic force that shapes reality. Some believe that the phrase *abracadabra* originates from the Hebrew words *ebrah k'dabri*, meaning "I create as I speak."[2] This concept reminds us that every word spoken has an effect, influencing those around us and shaping the energy of our leadership.

In leadership, communication should always align with the principle: "Do no harm." Even small deceptions—whether white lies, half-truths, or manipulative speech—create an energetic distortion in the Throat Chakra. Suppressed expression (underactive) or distorted communication (overactive) accumulate over time, unraveling one's connection to truth and trustworthiness. The 17th-century proverb, "cheaters never prosper," has persisted for a reason—dishonest words will always return to their source, often with unintended consequences.

Underactive Throat Chakra: Hesitation, Fear, and Self-Censorship

When leaders suppress their voices due to fear of rejection, judgment, or conflict, they create inner turmoil. This suppression often originates from a deep-rooted fear of exclusion, triggering survival instincts linked to the Root Chakra. Leaders who avoid difficult conversations, withhold feedback to maintain approval, or struggle to assert themselves ultimately weaken their authority, leading to:

- Unclear Direction: Employees struggle with ambiguity, lack of clear direction, and unresolved tensions, reducing morale and productivity.
- Avoidance of Confrontation: A "yes-man" culture, where employees hesitate to offer fresh perspectives or challenge the status quo.
- Lack of Presence: The leader being perceived as passive, soft-spoken, or lacking confidence, reducing trust and credibility.
- Over-Reliance on Approval: Seeking external validation before making decisions.
- Physical Discomfort: Throat issues, jaw tension, thyroid imbalances, and neck or shoulder pain can be a reflection of unspoken burdens a leader carries.

Overactive Throat Chakra: Over-Communication, Control, and Emotional Reactivity

Conversely, an overactive Throat Chakra can cause leaders to dominate conversations, dismiss input, or speak without emotional awareness. These leaders often believe they must control discussions to maintain authority, but this excessive communication can create frustration. Leaders with an overactive Throat Chakra may:

- Speak excessively without listening, leaving little space for others to contribute and overloading teams with information rather than fostering meaningful dialogue.
- Use intimidation, micromanaging tendencies, sharp criticism, or authoritative tones that create an unsafe space for team members to voice concerns and prevent team autonomy.
- Over-justify their actions, seeking external validation rather than standing in self-assured authenticity.

- Teams may withdraw, disengage, or fear speaking up, creating a culture of silence and compliance rather than innovation.
- Employees second-guess themselves, leading to delayed decision-making and a lack of trust in leadership.
- The leader may be perceived as controlling, unapproachable, or resistant to feedback, damaging psychological safety and collaboration.

Another manifestation of an imbalanced Throat Chakra is gossiping and chronic complaining. Both distort communication by focusing on negative energy rather than constructive solutions:

- Spreading rumors or discussing others behind their backs diminishes trust and unity. It entangles the leader's energy with negativity, lowering workplace morale and fostering division.
- A leader who constantly points out problems without offering solutions creates an environment of pessimism and frustration rather than innovation and progress.
- Habitual gossip or complaining pulls a leader into a low-frequency state, attracting more negativity and workplace discord.

When communication is overactive, the message gets lost in the noise. Hence, a balanced Throat Chakra is essential for effective leadership, as communication serves as a tool for vision, trust, and empowerment. Effective leaders understand the power of their voice—not to overpower, but to uplift; not to dictate, but to inspire. While the Throat Chakra is the energetic center of truth, it is not just personal truth—it is capital "T" Truth, rooted in divine wisdom and authenticity. It is easy to speak from the small "s" self—the conditioned mind, shaped by experiences, wounds, and insecurities. True Leadership, however, requires tapping into the Higher Self—the unchanging essence of who you are beyond external roles and expectations. For capital "T" Truth to genuinely be spoken by a leader, it must be rooted in radical authenticity and honesty. As such, it requires an open heart center for such honesty to be delivered with compassion, even when difficult conversations arise.

A mindful leader chooses words with intention, understanding that energy flows where attention goes. The workplace culture they create is a reflection of their communication style. Speaking and listening are two poles of the same energy, and true communication requires balance between both—for the one who listens is the one who knows. When leaders operate from a fully aligned Throat Chakra and rise above their shadows, they do not impose their voice onto others nor do they remain silent out of fear.

Throat Chakra Leadership Energy Meter

Before you begin, take a moment to pause and take three deep breaths—in through your nose, into your belly, and out through your mouth. As you answer each question, mark your responses in the space provided. Your responses will reveal your leadership energy in each category, and your overall Throat Chakra energy will be determined by patterns across all four categories.

Category 1: Clarity and Authentic Expression	Not Often (Underactive)	Just Right (Balanced)	Too Often (Overactive)
I restate or elaborate on my points to ensure they are fully understood.	☐	☐	☐
I share my opinions and feel the need to clarify.	☐	☐	☐
I actively contribute to discussions and take the lead in conversations.	☐	☐	☐
Category 1 Result:			

Category 2: Active Listening and Psychological Safety	Not Often (Underactive)	Just Right (Balanced)	Too Often (Overactive)
I speak more than I listen in team discussions.	☐	☐	☐
I step in to clarify or refine what others are trying to express.	☐	☐	☐
I am considered the loud or boisterous one in the team.	☐	☐	☐
Category 2 Result:			

Category 3: Constructive Feedback and Conflict Resolution	Not Often (Underactive)	Just Right (Balanced)	Too Often (Overactive)
I take an active role in guiding conflict resolution within my team.	☐	☐	☐

(Continued)

I make sure my perspective is heard when disagreements arise.	☐	☐	☐
I provide frequent, critical, and detailed feedback to my team members.	☐	☐	☐

Category 3 Result:

Category 4: Communication Patterns and Verbal Expression	Not Often (Underactive)	Just Right (Balanced)	Too Often (Overactive)
I keep conversations flowing without extended silences.	☐	☐	☐
I take the initiative to steer conversations in group discussions.	☐	☐	☐
I engage in discussions and contribute throughout conversations.	☐	☐	☐

Category 4 Result:

Decoding Your Energy Patterns: Throat Chakra Leadership

Category-Level Interpretation

- **Two or more "Not Often"** (Underactive): Hesitancy in communication, difficulty asserting viewpoints, or reluctance to engage in crucial conversations.
- **Two or more "Too Often"** (Overactive): Dominating discussions, over-explaining, or struggling to create space for others' input, leading to potential micromanagement.
- **Two "Just Right" + one other**: Mostly aligned but may need refinement in balancing self-expression with active listening.
- **All three "Just Right"**: Strong clarity and communication awareness, balancing assertiveness with receptivity.
- **One response in each**: Fluctuating communication style, signaling inconsistency in expression, listening, or feedback delivery.

Overall Throat Chakra Energy Interpretation

- **Three or more categories in one state**: Strong tendency toward that energy, indicating consistent communication patterns and potential blind spots in leadership style.
- **Two categories in one state + two mixed**: A dominant communication pattern with occasional shifts in clarity, listening, or engagement.
- **Two underactive + two overactive**: Shifting between excessive talking and withholding communication, requiring intentional recalibration for consistency.
- **Two underactive + two balanced**: Stability in some areas but a struggle with assertiveness, verbal confidence, or engaging in open dialogue.
- **Two overactive + two balanced**: Strong communicative presence but potential overextension, difficulty allowing space for others, or risk of overwhelming conversations.
- **Incoherent energetic states (no clear pattern)**: Highly adaptable, but frequent shifts in expression may signal instability, communication fatigue, or a need for verbal energy regulation.

Restoring Balance: Strategies for Clear, Intentional, and Authentic Communication

A well-balanced Throat Chakra empowers leaders to communicate with clarity, integrity, and EI. When balanced, leaders inspire trust, foster open dialogue, and create workplaces where every voice is valued. However, sustaining this balance requires self-awareness, intentional practice, and emotional discipline. The following strategies offer practical steps to restore balance, ensuring that leadership communication remains effective across both structured and intuitive approaches.

Action Steps to Balance an Underactive Throat Chakra

Strengthening Communication Confidence (Masculine: Assertion | Feminine: Authenticity)

- **Masculine Approach**: Practice direct and assertive speech by engaging in structured communication exercises, such as leading discussions or presenting ideas clearly in meetings.
- **Feminine Approach**: Cultivate authenticity by embracing vulnerability—allowing your true thoughts and feelings to surface in communication rather than holding back due to fear of rejection.

* **Example**: Begin each meeting with a clear and intentional message about objectives and vision. Encourage your team to do the same, fostering a culture where everyone's voice matters.

Encouraging Open and Transparent Dialogue (Masculine: Structure | Feminine: Openness)

* **Masculine Approach**: Establish regular team discussions where employees can express ideas and concerns in a structured setting.
* **Feminine Approach**: Foster psychological safety by demonstrating openness, validating others' perspectives, and actively listening without interruption.
* **Example**: Introduce an "open forum" practice, where employees can voice their thoughts in a judgment-free space, ensuring that feedback is valued and communication flows freely.

Speaking with Clarity and Purpose (Masculine: Precision | Feminine: Expressiveness)

* **Masculine Approach**: Focus on delivering concise and purposeful messages, eliminating unnecessary words or hesitation in speech.
* **Feminine Approach**: Infuse warmth and connection into communication, ensuring that messages are not just heard but felt.
* **Example**: Before responding to a question or making an important statement, pause and ensure your words align with your leadership values and intentions.

Action Steps to Balance an Overactive Throat Chakra

Practicing Active Listening and Discernment (Masculine: Restraint | Feminine: Receptivity)

* **Masculine Approach**: Exercise restraint in speaking by ensuring that dialogue is a two-way process, rather than dominating conversations.
* **Feminine Approach**: Cultivate deep listening skills, allowing space for others to express themselves fully before responding.
* **Example**: In meetings, challenge yourself to listen fully before responding. Implement a "pause before speaking" rule to encourage thoughtful and intentional communication.

Regulating Speech and Avoiding Over-Explanation (Masculine: Brevity | Feminine: Mindful Expression)

- **Masculine Approach**: Keep communication concise and avoid over-explaining or filling silence with unnecessary details.
- **Feminine Approach**: Embrace silence as a communication tool rather than feeling the need to fill every gap in conversation.
- **Example**: Before responding, ask yourself: "Is this necessary? Is this clear? Is this *constructive*?" If the answer is no, refine your message for maximum impact.

Cultivating Thoughtful and Constructive Feedback (Masculine: Directness | Feminine: Emotional Sensitivity)

- **Masculine Approach**: Deliver direct, structured feedback with clarity and confidence.
- **Feminine Approach**: Ensure that feedback is delivered with EI, balancing honesty with empathy.
- **Example**: When providing feedback, frame the conversation around growth rather than critique. Encourage employees to reflect on their own strengths and areas for improvement.

The words we speak shape the energy of our leadership. A balanced Throat Chakra allows leaders to use communication as a tool for empowerment, inspiration, and trust-building. However, balance does not come from speaking more or speaking less—it comes from ensuring that every word spoken is intentional, purposeful, and aligned with truth.

Moreover, leadership communication is not just about what is said but how it is received. A truly effective leader understands that communication is a dynamic process—one that requires both assertion and receptivity, expression and silence, and direction and openness. Restoring balance in the Throat Chakra is not a one-time effort—it is an ongoing journey of deep listening, intentional speaking, and authentic expression.

When leaders master the balance of communication, they don't just lead with authority; they lead with impact. They don't just speak; they inspire.

References

1. Elkins, D., Rueckert, C. L., & McCarty, J. A. (2018). *The Ra contact: Teaching the law of one* (Vol. 1). L/L Research.
2. Metcalfe, T. (2024, March 1). *The ancient—and mysterious—history of 'abracadabra'*. National Geographic. https://www.nationalgeographic.com/premium/article/abracadabra-meaning-malaria-spell-magic

Chapter 9

Third Eye Chakra

Visionary Leadership and Intuition

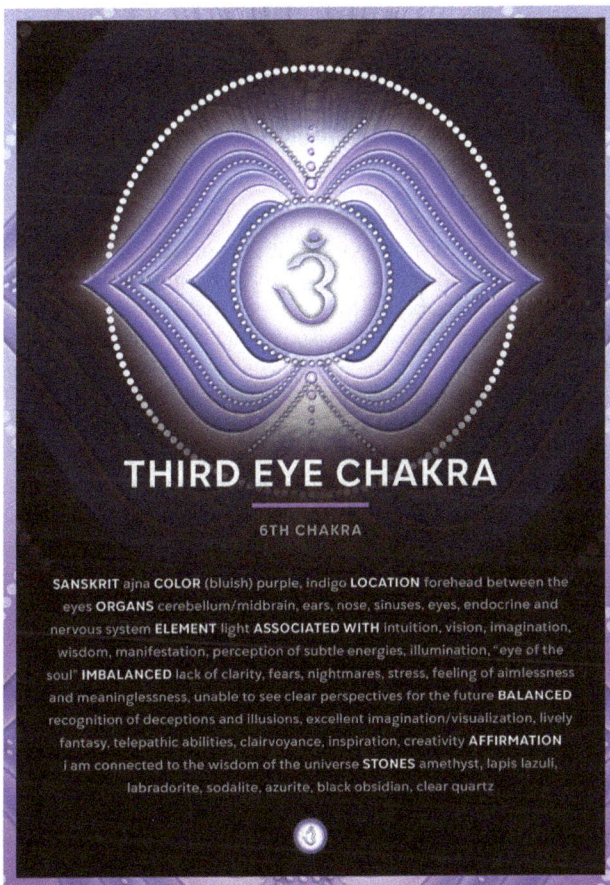

THIRD EYE CHAKRA

6TH CHAKRA

SANSKRIT ajna COLOR (bluish) purple, indigo LOCATION forehead between the eyes ORGANS cerebellum/midbrain, ears, nose, sinuses, eyes, endocrine and nervous system ELEMENT light ASSOCIATED WITH intuition, vision, imagination, wisdom, manifestation, perception of subtle energies, illumination, "eye of the soul" IMBALANCED lack of clarity, fears, nightmares, stress, feeling of aimlessness and meaninglessness, unable to see clear perspectives for the future BALANCED recognition of deceptions and illusions, excellent imagination/visualization, lively fantasy, telepathic abilities, clairvoyance, inspiration, creativity AFFIRMATION i am connected to the wisdom of the universe STONES amethyst, lapis lazuli, labradorite, sodalite, azurite, black obsidian, clear quartz

Source: iStock.com/Nicole Marte

DOI: 10.4324/9781003635918-10

In Steve Jobs' 2005 Stanford University commencement speech, he left the graduates with a message: "Have the courage to follow your heart and intuition. They somehow already know what you truly want to become. Everything else is secondary."

Jobs, the visionary founder of Apple, revolutionized the way we interact with technology, blending artistry and beauty with function and engineering. While known for his relentless pursuit of innovation, Jobs was also a deeply spiritual thinker, heavily influenced by Eastern philosophy. As a teenager, he read *Autobiography of a Yogi* by Paramahansa Yogananda—a book that later became his last gift to those in attendance at his funeral. At just 19, he embarked on a journey to India in search of enlightenment, immersing himself in the wisdom of meditation and Vedic teachings.[1]

Jobs was not alone in his reverence for intuition. Some of the most influential leaders of the modern world—Oprah Winfrey, Jeff Bezos, and Richard Branson—all speak about the power of trusting their instincts when making critical decisions. They understand that while data and logic provide structure, true wisdom often manifests in moments of intuitive clarity—a knowing that surpasses intellectual analysis.

So what exactly is intuition?

It is not guesswork or random instinct—it is direct perception of absolute Truth. It is a deep awareness of reality, beyond the distractions of the material world. When leaders develop their intuitive faculties, they are able to perceive patterns before they emerge, make decisions with clarity and conviction, and lead with wisdom that transcends conventional knowledge. Intuition lives in the land beyond senses, intellect, or reason. It is a direct plug into the vibrations of cosmic energy.

In Kantian philosophy, this distinction is made clear through the concepts of noumena and phenomena. The physical world we perceive—numbers, data points, business metrics—is phenomena and the outward manifestation of deeper energetic forces. Noumena, on the other hand, represents reality as it truly is—unfiltered by our senses, biases, or preconditioned thinking.[2] To understand this, think of a vast ocean with cresting waves. The ocean is the noumena, the pure substance of water. The wavelets we see on the ocean's surface are analogous to phenomena. These ever-changing cresting and falling waves that we observe at any given moment are but a tiny aspect of the vastness and depth that the ocean is in its totality. The same can be considered in Thomas Young's 1801 double-slit experiment which is widely cited as the demonstration that light and matter can exhibit the behavior of both classical particles and classical waves.[3]

The great visionary leaders operate from the level of connection to the noumena. They don't just see what is in front of them; they sense what is coming and position themselves accordingly. Similarly, modern physics has shown that what we call reality is largely an illusion—matter is made of energy, vibrating at different frequencies. As Sir Arthur Eddington noted, "the world we see and experience in everyday life is simply a convenient mirage."[4] What appears solid is actually an intricate dance of energy waves and empty space.

This understanding reinforces why leadership must evolve beyond the purely material and analytical—into the realm of energy, intuition, and inner alignment. Intuition is therefore the voice of the soul. It is the innate ability to discern reality, gain wisdom, and connect with the divine truth behind all veils of *māyā* (Sanskrit for illusion). Intuition is not contradictory to reason. It includes it, and is above it. Similar to how the second dimension is only a snapshot of the third dimension (where depth is added), reason is but a snapshot within the vast omniscient realm of intuition.

Intuition, in the chakra world, is governed by the Third Eye Chakra. It is the energetic center responsible for foresight, clarity, and wisdom. Located in the center of the forehead, between the eyebrows, this chakra is symbolized by an indigo-colored lotus with two petals, representing the merging of duality into a unified vision. When fully activated, the Third Eye is the gateway to higher perception—allowing leaders to see beyond surface-level reality and make decisions that align with long-term vision and purpose. This is why the greatest leaders of our time don't just react to trends—they anticipate them. They sense shifts before they happen, not because of spreadsheets or data models, but because their intuition allows them to read between the lines, perceive subtle patterns, and trust in the unseen.

To develop Third Eye leadership, one must cultivate the inner stillness necessary to hear intuition. Meditation, breathwork, visualization, and energy-based practices all play a role in strengthening this connection. Most importantly, the more one trusts their inner wisdom, the more intuitive guidance becomes second nature.

In leadership science, the qualities associated with the Third Eye Chakra—intuition, foresight, and visionary thinking—align closely with the Transformational Leadership theory. James MacGregor Burns, the pioneer of the Transformational Leadership Theory, describes transformational leaders as those who see beyond the immediate challenges, elevate their teams' thinking, and create a shared vision that ignites passion and commitment.[5] These leaders tap into something deeper than KPIs and metrics; they understand patterns, anticipate shifts, and make strategic decisions that align with long-term purpose.

When the Third Eye Chakra is open and balanced, leaders embody the core pillars of transformational leadership:

- **Visionary Thinking**: They look beyond short-term metrics and immediate obstacles, crafting a bigger-picture strategy that inspires long-term success.
- **Inner Trust and Decision-Making**: They rely on their intuition as much as their intellect, trusting their inner guidance even when the external environment is uncertain.

- **Innovative Problem-Solving**: They don't follow conventional paths; instead, they embrace nonlinear thinking, creativity, and bold new ideas that push boundaries.
- **Empowerment and Inspiration**: They encourage their teams to think beyond what is, toward what is possible—fostering a culture of innovation and high performance.
- **Authenticity and Alignment**: They lead from a place of deep self-awareness, ensuring that their words, actions, and vision align with their true purpose.

This is the power of CL—where intuition, strategy, and visionary leadership converge to create businesses, teams, and organizations that thrive not just in numbers, but in purpose and collective evolution.

Utilizing intuition can help the Chakra Leader adapt to changing situations calmly. Life on this physical plane of phenomena is constantly changing. Change is the nature of matter, changeless is the nature of Spirit. Therefore, in order to attune with the changeless intuition inherent in your soul, you must use the science of mindfulness in leadership. Meditation, visualization, and deep reflection are not soft skills. They are the tools that create clarity, resilience, and wisdom—the pillars of truly impactful leadership.

When the leadership of an organization creates a conscious space to look within for the answers, they can learn how to solve problems and projects instantaneously. Beyond this, they receive wisdom rooted in absolute Truth. The result is a management team that operates from divinely led inspiration, as opposed to solely egoic motivations. When this alignment is reached, the Third Eye of the individuals and organization is wide open. Gone are the days of reactivity and putting out fires; here to stay are the days of proactivity and acting on divinely downloaded inspiration.

We are at an evolution in leadership strategy. Just as Artificial Intelligence (AI) is driving the next technological revolution, human well-being and conscious leadership are driving the next leadership transformation. The leaders of tomorrow will not be those who simply manage tasks, analyze data, or execute strategies. They will be those who master energy, intuition, and alignment—those who recognize that leadership is not just about external results, but about internal mastery. In these changing times, energy is the new currency. How a leader manages their own energy directly impacts the energy of their team, their organization, and their community. The leaders who will thrive are those who understand that vision is not just about looking forward—it is about tuning inward. You are the Chief Energy Officer of your life, your team, and your company.

So now the question for you is: will you continue leading from the surface or will you step into your full power as a visionary leader? Your ability to lead from the Third Eye Chakra will define your impact.

Light Side: Visionary Leadership and Intuitive Mastery

Philosophers have long debated the question of free will—whether humans are truly autonomous or bound by fate. From a spiritual perspective, free will is not just the ability to make choices but the choice to align personal will with Divine Will. This requires stepping beyond the ego's desires, fears, and attachments and instead listening to the intuitive voice of the soul—the inner guidance system that knows our highest path.

True intuition often defies logic. It whispers in moments of silence, nudging us toward decisions that may seem irrational, impractical, or even uncomfortable. It may call us to leave behind stability for the unknown, to embrace uncertainty with faith, or to take a step that others perceive as reckless—yet within, there is an undeniable sense of trust, a knowing beyond reason.

To add more context, let us share with you a time when Neal transitioned from his corporate career, leaving behind a vice president title at Goldman Sachs—along with the prospect of managing director positions and million-dollar salaries—many considered his decision unfathomable. After all, he had spent decades working toward that pinnacle of corporate success. Yet, through devotional daily meditation, deep self-inquiry, and an unwavering connection to his inner guidance, he trusted the call to step into service through coaching and healing. While the external world may have viewed this choice as irrational, the inner world told a different story—one of alignment, authenticity, and higher purpose. This is the essence of the Chakra Leader with an open Third Eye: they do not make decisions based on external validation, but from an inner truth that is unwavering and deeply connected to the highest good.

This ability to clearly perceive beyond the tangible and into the unseen is the mark of a balanced Third Eye Chakra. There are no myopic focuses, but rather their awareness extends infinitely and is entrenched with razor-sharp perception. Almost as if they can see into the soul of the individual they're across from or have prophetic insights into the future. It is believed that as one elevates their level of consciousness, they begin to have fewer and fewer thoughts. The chatter from the little egoic voice in the head becomes quiet, and the individual begins to operate from a space of their Higher Self, where they are the ever-present observer, ready to take conscious action when needed.

The strengths and exemplary traits of the light side of the chakra leader in truthful communion with their Third Eye Chakra are those of heightened extra-sensory EI, inspiration, creativity, and, of course, intuition. There are no shortcuts to this level of consistent intuitive perception. While tools such as psychedelic and plant medicines can offer the ability to create new neurological pathways through neuroplasticity and rewiring one's brain, this short-term solution is merely window-shopping. The real way to step into the store and marvel at all it has within it is to go within yourself through daily meditation. The ancient and yogic science of meditation and kriya yoga are at the core of some of the most consistent tools used for millennia to develop deep intuition.

Many spiritual and mythological figures exemplify the power of insight, prophecy, and divine wisdom. These figures represent the highest expression of the Third Eye Chakra, offering guidance, vision, and the ability to see beyond surface-level reality.

- **Shiva (Hindu Mythology)**: In Hindu tradition, Lord Shiva's Third Eye represents pure perception and the destruction of illusion. When opened, it sees through falsehoods and reveals the absolute truth. Leaders who channel this energy are unshaken by external distractions and remain focused on their higher mission.
- **Tezcatlipoca (Aztec Mythology)**: In Aztec mythology, Tezcatlipoca, meaning "Smoking Mirror," was the god of foresight, destiny, and transformation. He was said to hold a mystical obsidian mirror that reflected both the hidden truths of the world and the illusions that deceived humanity. Leaders who embody Tezcatlipoca's wisdom possess the ability to see through illusions, recognize blind spots, and anticipate future shifts with clarity.
- **Huangdi (Chinese Mythology)**: Huangdi, the legendary Yellow Emperor, is revered in Taoist tradition as a master of strategy, innovation, and enlightenment. He is credited with establishing the foundations of Chinese medicine, governance, and philosophy. Huangdi's deep understanding of cosmic order and balance allowed him to govern wisely, integrating spiritual insight with practical leadership. He teaches leaders to combine logic with intuition, ensuring that decisions are not only strategic but also aligned with the greater good.

Mythological figures remind us that leaders with a balanced Third Eye Chakra can see beyond immediate obstacles, guiding their teams toward a visionary future. Like these legends, intuitive leaders access higher awareness, revealing truths beyond conventional perception. In modern organizations, this means tapping into insights to navigate challenges, anticipate shifts, and inspire transformation—aligning actions with a deeper purpose.

Balancing masculine and feminine energies, these leaders merge rational thought with intuitive insight, blending strategy with visionary creativity. They navigate uncertainty with confidence, ensuring short-term actions and long-term goals align with a greater mission. True intuitive leadership requires not just intelligence but a conscious surrender to higher wisdom, embracing change as a catalyst for growth and evolution.

Shadow Side: Overthinking, Clouded Judgment, and Loss of Vision in Leadership

Without balance in the Third Eye Chakra, leaders may struggle with clarity, foresight, and intuitive decision-making. Instead of embodying transformational leadership, where vision inspires and guides teams, leaders become transactional—focused solely on short-term metrics rather than long-term impact. When intuition is ignored, or worse, when ego overshadows insight, leadership becomes either rigidly analytical or blindly idealistic, leading to misalignment, stagnation, and disempowered teams. The shadow side of imbalance in this center can also appear as overthinking, having clouded judgment, or feeling a lack of self-trust. Beneath these leadership challenges lie deep-seated fears, limiting beliefs, and unexamined shadows that distort intuition and decision-making.

1 **Fear of the Unknown**

- Leaders who resist uncertainty and ambiguity cling to rigid structures, struggling to adapt to change or trust intuition.
- They over-rely on control and micromanagement, stifling creativity and strategic thinking within their teams.

2 **Ego and The Illusion of Certainty**

- Some leaders become so convinced of their own perspective that they disregard alternative viewpoints.
- This blocks collaborative innovation and creates a closed feedback loop, where only information that supports their existing beliefs is acknowledged.

3 **Attachment to External Validation**

- Leaders who lack inner clarity rely on external opinions and immediate results, shifting strategies based on short-term pressures rather than long-term vision.
- This leads to inconsistent leadership, where teams feel adrift and uninspired.

These shadows can present themselves in two ways: overactivity (overanalyzing, rigid thinking, and delusions of grandeur) or underactivity (lack of direction, confusion, and reliance on external validation).

Overactive Third Eye Chakra: The Detached Visionary

- Leaders with an overactive Third Eye often fixate on grand ideas without grounding them in reality. They may be seen as aloof, disconnected from team concerns, and overly focused on abstract concepts that lack tangible execution.
- This can manifest as analysis paralysis, where decisions are constantly debated but rarely acted upon.
- Employees may feel disillusioned, as their leader seems to live in ideas rather than engage with the realities of the business.
- An imbalanced Third Eye creates an over-reliance on logic, where leaders dismiss intuitive insights and creativity as impractical.
- Decision-making becomes cold, mechanical, and overly data-driven, leaving little room for bold, innovative thinking.
- Employees may feel disempowered to contribute ideas, as workplace culture values rigid structure over visionary problem-solving.

Underactive Third Eye Chakra: The Reactive Leader

- When the Third Eye is blocked or weak, leaders become trapped in the present, unable to anticipate trends, think strategically, or trust their instincts.
- These leaders rely heavily on external validation, making decisions based on short-term results, shareholder pressure, or fleeting trends rather than a clear long-term vision.
- The workplace lacks innovation and inspiration, as employees are simply executing tasks rather than contributing to a larger purpose.
- Without a strong inner compass, leaders constantly second-guess themselves, delaying decisions, and leading from a place of fear rather than confidence.
- Teams struggle with misalignment because leadership is inconsistent, frequently changing direction based on external pressures rather than an anchored vision.
- Employees feel uncertain about the company's future, reducing engagement and motivation.

An imbalanced Third Eye Chakra can leave leaders feeling directionless, stuck in reactive cycles, and unable to see the bigger picture. They become driven by external crises rather than long-term strategy. Over time, societal and workplace conditioning stifles intuitive thinking, prioritizing logic and measurable outcomes over creativity and vision. This limits a leader's ability to access new insights, crucial for effective decision-making. Cultivating a balanced Third Eye Chakra helps leaders move beyond short-term fixes, anticipate opportunities, and guide their teams with clarity and foresight.

Third Eye Chakra Leadership Energy Meter

Before you begin, take a moment to pause and take three deep breaths—in through your nose, into your belly, and out through your mouth. As you answer each question, mark your responses in the space provided. Your responses will reveal your leadership energy in each category, and your overall Third Eye Chakra energy will be determined by patterns across all four categories.

Category 1: Vision and Strategic Foresight	Not Often (Underactive)	Just Right (Balanced)	Too Often (Overactive)
I dedicate time to long-term strategy and future planning before making key decisions.	☐	☐	☐
I focus on future possibilities, sometimes losing sight of present realities.	☐	☐	☐
I emphasize connecting daily work to long-term goals with my team.	☐	☐	☐
Category 1 Result:			

Category 2: Strategic Awareness and Intuition	Not Often (Underactive)	Just Right (Balanced)	Too Often (Overactive)
I analyze extensive data and multiple perspectives before making decisions.	☐	☐	☐

(Continued)

I rely heavily on intuition when making decisions, even when data is available.	☐	☐	☐
I look for deeper meaning and patterns in situations.	☐	☐	☐

Category 2 Result:

Category 3: Discernment and Thought Patterns	Not Often (Underactive)	Just Right (Balanced)	Too Often (Overactive)
I process multiple perspectives and ideas at once, rather than focus on key priorities.	☐	☐	☐
I analyze leadership interactions in depth, sometimes replaying conversations in my mind.	☐	☐	☐
I reflect deeply on decisions, revisiting them even after they've been made.	☐	☐	☐

Category 3 Result:

Category 4: Creativity and Perspective Expansion	Not Often (Underactive)	Just Right (Balanced)	Too Often (Overactive)
I ask my team to take creative risks, even when the outcome is uncertain.	☐	☐	☐
I deeply explore abstract concepts before narrowing them into concrete strategies.	☐	☐	☐
I explore new possibilities before considering practical constraints.	☐	☐	☐

Category 4 Result:

Decoding Your Energy Patterns: Third Eye Chakra Leadership

Category-Level Interpretation

- **Two or more "Not Often"** (**Underactive**): Struggles with long-term vision, difficulty thinking strategically, or relies too heavily on external input instead of trusting intuition. May focus on short-term solutions over big-picture leadership.
- **Two or more "Too Often"** (**Overactive**): Overanalyzes decisions, gets lost in abstract thinking, or struggles to translate vision into action. May become disconnected from team concerns or stuck in theoretical problem-solving.
- **Two "Just Right" + one other**: Mostly aligned but may need refinement in balancing intuition with practical execution.
- **All three "Just Right"**: Strong ability to balance visionary leadership with logical execution, ensuring both strategy and action are aligned.
- **One response in each**: Fluctuating energy, signaling inconsistency in strategic thinking, intuitive decision-making, or the ability to balance vision with execution.

Overall Third Eye Chakra Energy Interpretation

- **Three or more categories in one state**: Strong tendency toward that energy, indicating leadership patterns and potential blind spots.
- **Two categories in one state + two mixed**: A dominant cognitive pattern with occasional instability in decision-making or visionary execution.
- **Two underactive + two overactive**: Swinging between overanalyzing and lack of strategic foresight, requiring intentional recalibration.
- **Two underactive + two balanced**: Stability in some areas but a struggle with long-term vision, intuitive trust, or abstract thinking.
- **Two overactive + two balanced**: Strong strategic thinking but potential for over-analysis, impractical ideas, or difficulty grounding vision into reality.
- **Incoherent energetic states (no clear pattern)**: Highly adaptable, but frequent shifts in cognitive engagement may signal instability, overthinking fatigue, or a need for improved decision-making balance.

Restoring Balance: Strategies for Visionary and Intuitive Leadership

For balanced Third Eye Chakra leadership, underactive tendencies require strengthening vision and trusting intuition, while overactive tendencies need grounding insights in practical strategies and avoiding over-analysis. Following strategies offer steps and insights to help restore balance, ensuring that visionary leadership remains effective and deeply aligned with purpose.

Action Steps to Balance an Underactive Third Eye Chakra

Cultivating Visionary Thinking and Expanding Perspective (Masculine: Strategic Foresight | Feminine: Intuitive Perception)

- **Masculine Approach**: Implement structured brainstorming sessions where teams analyze long-term trends and anticipate future challenges.
- **Feminine Approach**: Encourage intuitive thinking by incorporating visualization exercises or creative reflection techniques.
- **Example**: Host Vision Mapping Sessions where teams collectively visualize the company's trajectory over the next five years. Have each member write a letter from their future self, detailing the breakthroughs and innovations that shaped their success. This practice strengthens both strategic planning and intuitive insight.

Developing Trust in Intuition and Decision-Making (Masculine: Data-Driven Insights | Feminine: Inner Knowing)

- **Masculine Approach**: Use data analysis, market research, and strategic forecasting to support major decisions.
- **Feminine Approach**: Integrate mindfulness practices like meditation or reflective journaling to enhance inner clarity before making critical choices.
- **Example**: Before major leadership decisions, implement a "Pause & Align" ritual. Leaders take 5–10 minutes for deep breathing or guided meditation to tune into their intuition before reviewing the facts and figures. This allows decisions to be made with both clarity and confidence. Here is a meditation technique:

- Bring a problem or situation to mind without overthinking it—just let it be.
- Close your eyes, lift your gaze slightly, and take three slow, gentle breaths in and out, relaxing with each exhale. Sit quietly, clearing your mind and calming your heart. Feel the sacred, harmonious space within you, holding it with willpower.
- Now, bring the problem into this space and ask a broad question like, *What is the right thing to do?* or *What is my next step?* Listen with your heart, not your mind.
- Take another slow breath, exhale, and open your eyes, feeling the potential of your insight.
- If no clarity arises, write down your options and review them one by one, feeling for the choice that resonates. It may not make sense logically, but your intuition will guide you through the feeling of inner harmony.

Encouraging Open-Mindedness and Cognitive Flexibility
(Masculine: Rational Inquiry | Feminine: Expansive Thinking)

- **Masculine Approach**: Challenge existing assumptions by conducting regular "Why?" analyses, pushing teams to question outdated methods.
- **Feminine Approach**: Create space for curiosity by fostering cross-disciplinary learning and encouraging perspectives outside traditional industry norms.
- **Example**: Introduce "Reverse Brainstorming"—instead of asking how to solve a problem, ask teams to brainstorm how they could *create* the problem. This technique forces teams to think beyond habitual solutions and unlock fresh, unconventional insights.

Action Steps to Balance an Overactive Third Eye Chakra

Grounding Visionary Insights in Practical Execution
(Masculine: Tactical Planning | Feminine: Discernment)

- **Masculine Approach**: Set structured goals and clear timelines to prevent excessive over-planning or aimless ideation.
- **Feminine Approach**: Refine discernment by identifying which insights are worth pursuing and which are distractions.

- **Example**: Implement "Vision to Action Roadmaps"—a structured process where each intuitive insight or visionary idea is mapped into actionable steps with clear deadlines. This prevents leaders from getting lost in abstract thinking without tangible results.

Balancing Rational Analysis with Intuitive Wisdom (Masculine: Analytical Reasoning | Feminine: Trust in Inner Guidance)

- **Masculine Approach**: Establish decision-making frameworks (e.g., pros/cons lists, risk assessments) to balance instinct with logic.
- **Feminine Approach**: Develop a practice of deep listening—to both internal intuition and external feedback from trusted advisors.
- **Example**: Before making a high-stakes decision, leaders conduct a "Logic & Intuition Check"—first writing down all logical reasons for a choice, then taking five minutes to sit in silence, allowing their inner wisdom to surface. This process ensures that decisions align with both reason and instinct.

Avoiding Overthinking and Analysis Paralysis (Masculine: Clarity and Decisiveness | Feminine: Trust and Flow)

- **Masculine Approach**: Limit decision-making cycles to avoid excessive rumination—set a deadline for finalizing choices.
- **Feminine Approach**: Cultivate a mindset of trust, recognizing that no decision is perfect and adapting as new insights emerge.
- **Example**: Introduce "Decision Windows"—leaders give themselves a set period (e.g., 48 hours) to gather insights, reflect, and make a firm decision. This prevents paralysis and encourages confidence in one's choices.

Leadership in the modern world is no longer just about solving problems—it's about seeing beyond them. Those who cultivate a balanced Third Eye Chakra become the visionaries who guide their organizations not just through the complexities of today but toward the unwritten possibilities of tomorrow. They are the ones who integrate logic with intuition, structure with creativity, and analysis with insight, shaping the future instead of merely reacting to it.

These leaders do not operate from fear, doubt, or rigid thinking. Instead, they trust their inner knowing, allowing them to navigate uncertainty with confidence and make bold decisions rooted in wisdom rather than worry. Their ability to perceive patterns, anticipate shifts, and align their leadership with a higher vision sets them apart as beacons of clarity in a world clouded by distraction.

But the truth is this: the more you see, the more you see.

As we move forward, the future of leadership will belong to those who see beyond what is and envision what could be in their mind's eye. With that, we leave you with a question to reflect. *In a world where many blindly follow, will you be the one who sees?*

References

1. Isaacson, W. (2011). *Steve Jobs*. Simon & Schuster.
2. Kant, I. (1781/1998). *Critique of pure reason* (P. Guyer & A. Wood, Trans.). Cambridge University Press.
3. Young, T. (1804). Experiments and calculations relative to physical optics. *Philosophical Transactions of the Royal Society of London, 94,* 1–16. https://doi.org/10.1098/rstl.1804.0001
4. Eddington, A. S. (1928). *The Nature of the physical world*. Cambridge University Press.
5. Burns, J. M. (1978). *Leadership*. Harper & Row.

Chapter 10

Crown Chakra

Purpose-Driven Leadership and Spiritual Connection

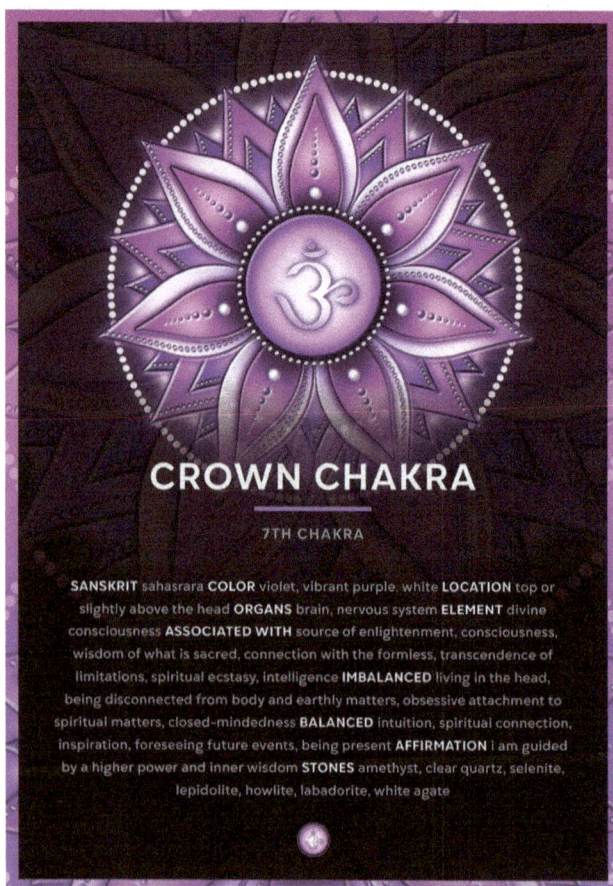

CROWN CHAKRA

7TH CHAKRA

SANSKRIT sahasrara **COLOR** violet, vibrant purple, white **LOCATION** top or slightly above the head **ORGANS** brain, nervous system **ELEMENT** divine consciousness **ASSOCIATED WITH** source of enlightenment, consciousness, wisdom of what is sacred, connection with the formless, transcendence of limitations, spiritual ecstasy, intelligence **IMBALANCED** living in the head, being disconnected from body and earthly matters, obsessive attachment to spiritual matters, closed-mindedness **BALANCED** intuition, spiritual connection, inspiration, foreseeing future events, being present **AFFIRMATION** I am guided by a higher power and inner wisdom **STONES** amethyst, clear quartz, selenite, lepidolite, howlite, labadorite, white agate

Source: iStock.com/Nicole Marte

DOI: 10.4324/9781003635918-11

Pause for a moment and close your eyes as you reflect on this question: "What does it mean to be truly present?"

Not just physically in the room, but fully aligned in mind, body, and spirit. Reflect on a time when you weren't caught up in past regrets or future anxieties—but when you were simply here, in the eternal now. That feeling is the essence of the Crown Chakra, the highest energetic center in the Chakra system. The Crown Chakra, often visualized as a 1,000-petaled lotus, represents our connection to Source consciousness—that universal energy that binds all life. Its violet-white light signifies oneness and wholeness, merging all aspects of our being into a unified field. Just as a white ray of light refracted through a prism reveals all colors of the rainbow, the Crown Chakra holds the essence of every other chakra within it. It's the masculine pole of the cosmos, balanced perfectly with the feminine grounding of the Root Chakra, tethering us to Mother Earth, known by many names such as Gaia or Pachamama across various traditions.

Yet here's the paradox: while the Crown connects us to limitless wisdom and universal consciousness, it also forces us to confront our deepest human struggles—the relentless pull of the ego. The ego craves control, certainty, and recognition, while the Crown asks us to surrender and trust in the unfolding of life without needing to have all the answers. This surrender isn't passive; it's a radical act of courage. The Crown teaches that true power lies not in external forces, but in your Higher Self and the intelligent flow of life. It's about trusting that even when things don't go according to your mental plan, you're exactly where you need to be. It's the realization that leadership isn't about pushing harder, but about aligning deeper. It's easy to strategize, to lead from intellect, or to rely on past experience. But to release control and trust in something unseen? That's the ultimate challenge and within—the ultimate liberation.

If we define reality as what we can experience through our five senses, the only moment that truly exists is the present. Everything else— memories of the past, projections into the future—is a construct of the mind. Think about that: the conversations you had yesterday or the plans you've made for tomorrow are mental phenomena, not tangible realities. The Crown Chakra reminds us that the eternal now is the only place where life—and leadership—truly unfolds. This presence opens the door to greater purpose in all actions. When leaders slow down to cultivate heightened presence, they are fully engaged in the moment, allowing them to respond to challenges with clarity and calmness.

But how often do we, as leaders, get pulled out of the now? Do you find yourself ruminating on past mistakes or replaying conversations you wish had gone differently? Or perhaps you're caught in anxiety about future outcomes, strategizing for scenarios that may not ever happen. Maybe you've been in meetings where you're crafting your next response while your team is still speaking, missing the opportunity to truly listen and connect. These are all signs of a Crown Chakra imbalance—where the mind's noise drowns out the wisdom of presence.

Imagine you're the CEO of a Fortune 500 company. You're on a live earnings call when a stock analyst challenges your decision to invest millions in new real estate that hasn't yet turned a profit. If your Crown Chakra is blocked by ego or fear, your mind might spiral—grasping for the perfect defense, worrying about investor reactions, or even feeling personally attacked. But if you've cultivated mindfulness and presence through Crown Chakra alignment, your response would be entirely different.

A Chakra Leader uses their breath to anchor themselves in the now, resisting the urge to react from fear or defensiveness. Instead, they listen deeply, feel into the question, and respond from a place of clarity, integrity, and higher purpose. This isn't about spinning a narrative to appease stakeholders; it's about embodying a frequency of leadership that resonates with truth. The vibration of your words, the calm in your tone, and the confidence in your energy become palpable to everyone on that call. That's not just good leadership—that's transformational leadership.

Light Side: Purpose-Driven Leadership and Divine Connection

At its highest expression, leadership through the Crown Chakra transcends mere authority—it becomes an act of purposeful service. The power of purpose is both a spiritual concept and one grounded in science. A 2016 study conducted by academic psychologists from Canada and the United States found that individuals with a strong sense of purpose not only reported higher levels of life satisfaction but also experienced tangible success, including higher household income and net worth, along with sustained growth in these areas over the following decade.[1] This underscores a fundamental truth: purpose fuels prosperity. When leaders are aligned with their deeper mission, it positively influences every aspect of their lives, including their careers and financial outcomes.

Leading with purpose represents the light side of the Chakra Leader who is balanced and connected to their Crown Chakra. Purpose arises from self-acceptance, living in authenticity, and following the passions that resonate deeply within. But there's an important distinction: passion is for you, while purpose is for others. Passion ignites personal fulfillment, but when that passion is directed in service to others, it transforms into purpose. This is where true leadership emerges—when personal gifts and talents are channeled to make a positive impact on the lives of others.

For leaders seeking to uncover or deepen their sense of purpose, the key lies in leveraging both their innate gifts and the skills cultivated throughout life. Helping others becomes a mirror—reflecting back insights into your own identity and growth. As this practice deepens, the leader begins to dissolve the egoic attachment to their role, recognizing that leadership is not about personal accolades but about being a vessel through which the Divine can work. In this state, leadership is no longer just a title—it is a calling, a sacred responsibility to guide others with wisdom, compassion, and purpose.

When passion meets service, and presence meets purpose, a leader becomes unstoppable—not because of their authority, but because they are in flow with the greater good.

Similarly, throughout history and mythology, leaders who embodied this divine connection were revered not for their power but for their ability to inspire, unify, and elevate the consciousness of their people. These mythological figures represent the light side of the Crown Chakra—leaders who balanced inner stillness with external action, personal purpose with collective upliftment.

- **King Solomon (Biblical and Abrahamic Traditions):** Known for his wisdom and deep connection to divine guidance, Solomon ruled with fairness and insight. He symbolizes the ability to receive and implement higher wisdom in leadership, making decisions that serve both justice and the greater good. Leaders who channel Solomon's energy lead from a place of inner stillness and clarity, ensuring their actions align with a higher moral compass.
- **Athena (Greek Mythology):** The Goddess of Wisdom, Strategic Warfare, and Justice, represents intellectual clarity combined with divine intuition. She teaches leaders to balance strategic planning with inspired insight, ensuring decisions are not only practical but deeply aligned with universal truths. Athena's energy reminds leaders that wisdom and fairness are the cornerstones of impactful leadership.
- **Vishnu (Hindu Mythology):** As the Preserver and Protector of the Universe, Vishnu embodies the harmonious balance between cosmic order and compassionate leadership. Leaders inspired by Vishnu's energy understand their role as guardians of balance, ensuring that their organizations thrive while maintaining ethical integrity and social responsibility.

When a leader is aligned or sometimes even said to be "in flow," with their higher purpose, their leadership becomes an act of service, not just to their organization but to humanity as a whole. Leaders who operate from a balanced Crown Chakra create workplaces where vision, clarity, and higher purpose guide every aspect of the organization. However, balancing the Crown Chakra requires integrating both masculine and feminine energies—the structured pursuit of goals (masculine) and the open, receptive connection to higher wisdom (feminine). This duality ensures that leaders remain grounded while staying connected to their higher purpose. The following is how the balance of masculine/feminine energies is attained and their resulting impact:

Masculine Approach: Structured Purpose and Strategic Vision

- Define Clear Organizational Values: Regularly revisit and articulate the core values and mission that guide your leadership and organizational decisions.
- Strategic Visioning Sessions: Implement structured, goal-oriented sessions that align daily operations with the organization's long-term purpose.
- Measure Purpose-Driven Impact: Use tangible metrics to assess how well the organization is aligning with its mission, ensuring that purpose is not lost in the day-to-day grind.

Feminine Approach: Receptivity, Intuition, and Universal Connection

- Meditation and Reflection Practices: Incorporate regular mindfulness practices to stay connected with your inner guidance and universal wisdom.
- Encourage Collective Purpose: Create opportunities for team members to share their personal connection to the organization's mission, fostering a shared sense of purpose.
- Embrace Surrender and Trust: Practice letting go of the need to control every outcome, trusting in the flow of divine guidance and the inherent wisdom of the team.

Impact Manifestation:

- Inspiration and Alignment: Teams feel deeply connected to the organization's mission, fostering a sense of purpose and motivation that transcends typical workplace engagement.
- Innovative Thinking: Leaders with a balanced Crown Chakra inspire visionary ideas and creative problem-solving, encouraging teams to think beyond conventional boundaries.

- Ethical Leadership: Decisions are guided by integrity and a higher sense of responsibility, ensuring that success is sustainable and aligned with universal values.
- Resilient Culture: A purpose-driven organization is more adaptable to change, as employees are anchored in shared values rather than fleeting trends.

As Viktor Frankl, renowned psychiatrist and Holocaust survivor, once said, "Those who have a 'why' to live can bear almost any 'how.'"[2] This truth speaks directly to Crown Chakra leadership. When leaders are anchored in their "why"—their higher purpose—they possess the resilience, vision, and clarity to navigate any challenge. Their leadership becomes not just a role, but a calling—one that transforms their organizations and, most importantly, themselves.

Shadow Side: Disconnection, Distrust, and the Crisis of Purpose

Unlike other chakras that govern more tangible aspects of leadership, the Crown Chakra deals with the most abstract and elusive: our sense of meaning and spiritual connection. This makes its shadows both harder to recognize and more difficult to confront, as they challenge the very foundation of our existence and leadership. At the core of the Crown Chakra imbalances lies a fear of the non-physical—a reluctance to embrace the spiritual, intuitive, and transcendent aspects of our being. Leaders, especially in the corporate and political realms, often shy away from acknowledging these dimensions because they defy conventional logic and can't be quantified on a balance sheet or spreadsheet.

Many high-performing leaders, despite their outward success, quietly wrestle with unexplained spiritual experiences—whether it's intuitive flashes, dreams that predict outcomes, or an unshakable sense of being guided by something beyond themselves. Yet because these experiences can't be controlled or rationalized, they're often suppressed or dismissed. This suppression creates an energetic condensation in the Crown Chakra, manifesting as a deep-seated discomfort with one's own spirituality. For someone new or unaccustomed to receiving these extrasensory perceptions, it can feel overwhelming or even contradictory to personal beliefs. As a result, the self-instruction becomes to shut this part down, so it lays dormant for years and decades; but these reminders of spiritual experiences never truly fade.

When leaders fear or reject this part of themselves, they become disconnected from their inner sovereign archetype—the King or Queen within.

This archetype represents the wise, just ruler who governs not just an external kingdom but the internal landscape of the psyche. Without a strong connection to this archetype, leaders lose their sense of order, vision, and purpose, causing their entire leadership style to become reactive and fragmented. They may excel at strategy and execution but struggle with meaning, fulfillment, and long-term vision. These internal imbalances cascade outward, influencing behavior, decision-making, and workplace culture.

Underactive Crown Chakra: Disconnection from Purpose and Vision

Leaders with an underactive Crown Chakra may feel disconnected from their higher purpose and lack a clear vision for their team or organization. They often rely solely on material success or external validation, neglecting the deeper meaning behind their work. This can create a mechanical, uninspired approach to leadership, where innovation stalls and the team feels directionless.

Symptoms of an underactive Crown Chakra:

- A sense of purposelessness or lack of inspiration in leadership decisions.
- Over-reliance on data and external validation, neglecting intuition and inner guidance.
- Difficulty connecting daily tasks to a larger mission, leading to team disengagement.
- **Example**: A leader who focuses solely on quarterly profits without considering the long-term vision or impact on the community may foster a culture of burnout, low team morale, disengagement, and a transactional work culture.

Overactive Crown Chakra: Over-Identification with Ego and Detachment from Reality

Leaders with an overactive Crown Chakra may become overly fixated on grand visions or personal enlightenment, to the point of detachment from practical realities. They may operate from a place of spiritual arrogance, believing their insights are superior, and disregarding feedback from others. This creates a disconnect between leadership and the team, leading to poor decision-making and a lack of grounded execution.

Symptoms of an overactive Crown Chakra:

- Grandiose thinking, with visions disconnected from actionable steps.
- Spiritual bypassing—using spirituality to avoid real-world challenges or difficult conversations.

- Dismissing team input, believing their vision alone is sufficient for success.
- **Example**: A leader who constantly focuses on "big-picture" ideas without considering the practical needs of the team may neglect critical operational details, leading to confusion and frustration. They may also alienate team members by dismissing their contributions in favor of their own perceived higher wisdom.

An imbalanced Crown Chakra can leave leaders feeling disconnected from purpose and clarity. An underactive Crown Chakra leads to a lack of vision, with leaders focused on short-term goals, causing team disengagement and a transactional work culture. Conversely, an overactive Crown Chakra fosters ego-driven leadership, where leaders dominate decisions, dismiss feedback, and stifle collaboration. Some may fall into spiritual bypassing, embracing abstract ideals without grounding them in action, leading to frustration and confusion within teams. Others may feel overwhelmed, becoming inconsistent or emotionally detached. At the root of these issues are fears of the unknown and a rejection of intuition, which limits creativity and authentic connection.

The path out of the Crown Chakra's shadow begins with radical self-awareness and embracing the unknown. Leaders must learn not to suppress their spiritual experiences but to integrate them into a holistic approach that balances intellect with intuition, structure with surrender, and ambition with higher purpose. This journey isn't about abandoning reason; it's about elevating leadership to a place where reason and faith coexist, where data-driven decisions are informed by inner knowing and where the pursuit of success is grounded in service and meaning.

As leaders reconnect with their divine purpose and spiritual guidance, they unlock personal transformation and also the potential to revolutionize their organizations. They cultivate workplaces that are inspired and resilient, capable of navigating uncertainty with ease and grace. For these reasons and more, creating balance in our Chakras is vital.

Crown Chakra Leadership Energy Meter

Before you begin, take a moment to pause and take three deep breaths—in through your nose, into your belly, and out through your mouth. As you answer each question, mark your responses in the space provided. Your responses will reveal your leadership energy in each category, and your overall Crown Chakra energy will be determined by patterns across all four categories.

Category 1: Big-Picture Thinking and Practical Leadership	Not Often (Underactive)	Just Right (Balanced)	Too Often (Overactive)
I focus on big-picture goals before execution.	☐	☐	☐
I feel strongly connected to a larger purpose.	☐	☐	☐
I provide direction for my team and make decisions independently.	☐	☐	☐
Category 1 Result:			

Category 2: Open-Mindedness and Perspective	Not Often (Underactive)	Just Right (Balanced)	Too Often (Overactive)
I consider multiple perspectives before making decisions.	☐	☐	☐
I let situations unfold without needing to control.	☐	☐	☐
I encourage new ways of thinking, even when they challenge existing structures.	☐	☐	☐
Category 2 Result:			

Category 3: Spiritual Connection and Grounding	Not Often (Underactive)	Just Right (Balanced)	Too Often (Overactive)
I feel connected to something greater than myself, such as a higher power, universal energy, or collective purpose.	☐	☐	☐
I incorporate energetic or spiritual practices to guide my decisions.	☐	☐	☐

(Continued)

	Not Often (Underactive)	Just Right (Balanced)	Too Often (Overactive)
I prioritize visionary thinking over daily leadership tasks.	☐	☐	☐

Category 3 Result:

Category 4: Ego and Humility	Not Often (Underactive)	Just Right (Balanced)	Too Often (Overactive)
I see leadership as a purpose, not a personal identity.	☐	☐	☐
I receive feedback but sometimes feel it doesn't apply to me.	☐	☐	☐
I recognize my strengths without feeling the need to prove myself.	☐	☐	☐

Category 4 Result:

Decoding Your Energy Patterns: Crown Chakra Leadership

Category-Level Interpretation

- **Two or more "Not Often" (Underactive):** Feels disconnected from purpose, struggles to find meaning in leadership, or relies too heavily on external validation. May focus on immediate tasks without considering long-term vision or higher wisdom.
- **Two or more "Too Often" (Overactive):** Detached from practical leadership, overly idealistic, or absorbed in abstract concepts without grounding them in action. May resist feedback, believing their vision alone is sufficient.
- **Two "Just Right" + one other:** Mostly aligned but may need refinement in balancing visionary thinking with day-to-day leadership responsibilities.
- **All three "Just Right":** Strong ability to integrate purpose with leadership execution, maintaining wisdom and practicality.
- **One response in each:** Fluctuating energy, signaling inconsistency in purpose-driven leadership, decision-making, or balance between vision and action.

Overall Crown Chakra Energy Interpretation

- **Three or more categories in one state:** Strong tendency toward that energy, shaping leadership style and potential blind spots.
- **Two categories in one state + two mixed:** A dominant leadership pattern with occasional instability in execution or alignment with purpose.
- **Two underactive + two overactive:** Shifting between detachment and lack of clarity, requiring intentional recalibration to maintain balance.
- **Two underactive + two balanced:** Stability in some areas but difficulty in trusting intuition, defining purpose, or sustaining visionary thinking.
- **Two overactive + two balanced:** Strong spiritual connection and vision but potential for impracticality, grandiosity, or avoidance of present realities.
- **Incoherent energetic states (no clear pattern):** Highly adaptable, but frequent shifts in leadership engagement may signal instability, burnout, or a need for better alignment between higher wisdom and grounded leadership.

Restoring Balance: Strategies for Purpose-Driven and Grounded Leadership

Restoring balance requires harmonizing the spiritual with the tangible, ensuring that leaders stay connected to their higher mission while remaining grounded in the everyday realities of leadership. The following practices offer approaches to balancing the Crown Chakra, guiding leaders to connect deeply with their purpose while maintaining clarity and focus in their daily leadership roles.

Action Steps to Balance an Underactive Crown Chakra

Reconnect with Your Higher Purpose (Masculine: Vision Mapping | Feminine: Inner Exploration)

- **Masculine Approach:** Create a *Purpose Map*—a visual roadmap that outlines your core values, long-term mission, and how your daily actions align with your higher purpose.
- **Feminine Approach:** Engage in *deep reflection* through meditation or journaling to explore the underlying "why" behind your leadership journey.

- **Example**: Host a Vision Retreat for yourself or your leadership team. Spend the day reflecting on your core values and organizational mission. Break this down into actionable goals, then reconnect with how each project serves a higher purpose. Use this process to align your team's efforts with long-term, meaningful objectives.

Crown Chakra Meditation for Spiritual Alignment (Masculine: Focused Intention | Feminine: Receptive Stillness)

- **Masculine Approach**: Set a clear intention before meditation, focusing on specific leadership challenges you wish to align with your higher purpose.
- **Feminine Approach**: Surrender to the flow of the meditation, allowing intuitive insights to arise naturally without forcing outcomes.
- **Example**: Begin your day with a Crown Chakra Meditation: Sit upright with a straight spine. Close your eyes and take three deep belly breaths. Focus your energy on your heart, connecting inward. Bring awareness to the crown of your head and feel a fine vibration or tingling sensation. Visualize a violet-white light of pure creative energy flowing into your crown. Allow this light to fill you with clarity, connecting you to the abundance of the Divine. As it flows through you, set an intention for your leadership—for wisdom, integrity, and service to the greater good. Let this light guide your day, anchoring your leadership in purpose and presence.

Foster Purpose-Driven Team Engagement (Masculine: Strategic Alignment | Feminine: Collective Connection)

- **Masculine Approach**: Ensure that every team member's role directly contributes to the organization's mission and purpose through structured goal-setting.
- **Feminine Approach**: Encourage personal reflections within the team on how their work aligns with their individual values and passions.
- **Example**: Introduce a Purpose Alignment activity during team meetings. Ask each team member to share how their current projects contribute to their personal growth and the organization's mission. This practice reinforces both individual and collective purpose, creating a stronger sense of meaning and engagement across the team.

Action Steps to Balance an Overactive Crown Chakra

Ground Visionary Thinking in Practical Execution (Masculine: Structured Planning | Feminine: Visionary Inspiration)

- **Masculine Approach**: Translate big-picture ideas into detailed action plans with clear milestones and timelines.
- **Feminine Approach**: Maintain space for creative inspiration but ensure it is balanced with actionable steps.
- **Example**: When inspired by a new idea, apply the Three-Tier Grounding Method:

  1 Write down the vision in its broadest form.
  2 Break the vision into three actionable goals that can be achieved within a realistic timeline.
  3 Assign specific tasks to yourself or your team to bring the vision to life. This process ensures that your ideas don't remain abstract but become tangible, executable plans.

Nature Walk Presence Exercise to Anchor Leadership (Masculine: Physical Grounding | Feminine: Mindful Observation)

- **Masculine Approach**: Use nature walks as a deliberate practice to reconnect with the physical world, anchoring visionary ideas into grounded reflection.
- **Feminine Approach**: Cultivate mindful presence, allowing nature to bring awareness to your thoughts and patterns without judgment.
- **Example**: Take a 10-minute nature walk with a focus on presence: As you walk, notice your surroundings without labeling or judging them. If a thought arises—whether related to work, personal life, or even the beauty of nature—pause for two seconds to acknowledge the thought, then continue walking. Over time, this practice helps reduce overactive mental chatter and strengthens your connection to the present moment, fostering clarity and grounded leadership.

Balance Detachment with Engaged Leadership (Masculine: Leadership Presence | Feminine: Servant Leadership)

- **Masculine Approach**: Stay actively engaged with your team's daily challenges and successes, offering practical support when needed.
- **Feminine Approach**: Approach leadership as a service, fostering a culture of humility, collaboration, and shared growth.

- **Example**: Implement Office Hours where team members can discuss their projects, challenges, or even personal aspirations. Use this time to stay connected to your team's realities, offering practical advice while maintaining an openness to their ideas and needs. This balances your visionary leadership with grounded, engaged presence.

It is not enough to have a compelling vision; leaders must integrate that vision with aligned actions, strategic thinking, and a sense of service. When leaders operate from this balanced state, they inspire their teams to innovate fearlessly, engage meaningfully, and contribute to something greater than themselves. Leaders operating from this space are deeply connected to their higher mission while remaining grounded in the realities of their teams and communities. They inspire innovation without losing touch with practicality, and they cultivate cultures that thrive on both strategic clarity and spiritual alignment.

But here's the deeper truth: leadership at this level isn't a title or position—it's a state of being. It's waking up every day with the intention to serve something greater than yourself, while having the discipline to translate that intention into tangible outcomes. It's balancing the invisible with the visible, the cosmic with the concrete.

As you continue this journey, recognize that the Crown Chakra isn't the final destination—it's the gateway to continuous evolution. Each moment of presence, each decision rooted in purpose, and each act of service ripples outward, shaping not just organizations but the very fabric of our collective consciousness.

Vision doesn't end at the horizon—it expands with every step you take. The future will be shaped by those leaders who dare to move beyond what is known, who trust their inner compass, and who lead from a place of aligned energy and unwavering clarity.

The question isn't whether you'll rise to meet this future—the question is, how brightly will you shine when you get there?

References

1. Hill, P. L., Turiano, N. A., Mroczek, D. K., & Burrow, A. L. (2016). The value of a purposeful life: Sense of purpose predicts greater income and net worth. *Journal of Research in Personality*, 65, 38–42. https://doi.org/10.1016/j.jrp.2016.07.003
2. Frankl, V. E. (1984). *Man's search for meaning: An introduction to logotherapy* (I. Lasch, Trans.). Beacon Press.

Chapter 11

Balancing the Chakras in Modern Leadership

- 🟣 I understand
- 🔵 I see
- 🟦 I speak
- 🟢 I love
- 🟡 I do
- 🟠 I feel
- 🔴 I am

Source: iStock.com/JulyProkopiv

Recognizing Imbalances: The First Step to Alignment

You glance at the clock. T-minus 15 minutes until one of the most critical client calls of your career. The pitch deck is open in front of you—your bespoke solution could redefine your industry, bringing a historic win for your company. But as you review your notes one last time, a familiar sensation sets in. Your heart pounds a little faster, your breath grows shallow, and your palms moisten against the mouse. The pressure to perform flawlessly in front of C-suite executives and your own leadership team brings a tightness to your chest and anxiety to your mind.

DOI: 10.4324/9781003635918-12

Life in the business world moves fast. Back-to-back meetings blur together, leaving little time for a proper lunch—let alone a moment to breathe. Energy is constantly exchanged in high-stress environments, and whether you realize it or not, the words, emotions, and even unspoken tensions of those around you seep into your own headspace. The frustration of a colleague after a difficult client interaction, the distracted chatter of junior analysts a few desks away, or the lingering stress from an unresolved conflict at home—these subtle energetic shifts impact your own mental state, your focus, and ultimately, your leadership presence.

Leaders feeling stuck, overwhelmed, or disconnected are often operating with unbalanced energy centers. Chakra Leaders who thrive in high-stress environments understand the importance of recognizing their imbalances and embracing energy management practices as recalibration tools. A simple five-minute breathing exercise before a high-stakes meeting, a grounding practice between calls, or a short moment of stillness before making a major decision can be the difference between scattered, reactive leadership and a composed, present, and intentional approach.

Energy Management Practices for High-Stress Environments

Energy management isn't a luxury—It's a necessity. Whether you're preparing for a big client presentation, navigating a difficult conversation with your team, or making critical decisions under pressure, the ability to regulate your energy can be the difference between reactive leadership and conscious, intentional decision-making. While traditional leadership development focuses on external strategies—delegation, productivity hacks, and time management—truly effective leadership starts from within.

During his last few years at Goldman Sachs, Neal experienced firsthand the power of these micropractices. At this time, a portion of a hallway-sized coat closet had been repurposed into a small prayer and contemplation room. With the relentless pace of meetings and tasks, there was often no time for breaks in the world of investment banking. However, Neal learned that even five minutes in this space, closing his eyes and consciously reconnecting with his breath, created a profound reset. These moments allowed him to enter client meetings with a clear mind, preventing external stress from clouding his leadership presence.

Similarly, Zohra found that the most resilient leaders she worked with were those who incorporated intentional energy practices into their routines. They weren't waiting for stress to overwhelm them before taking action—they were proactive, using grounding exercises, breathwork, and mindfulness techniques to maintain alignment throughout the day.

As we have shared in previous chapters, when a chakra is overactive or underactive due to shadows, these imbalances manifest in tangible workplace challenges, affecting both leaders and their teams. Here is a quick recap on imbalances, their impacts, and energy management practices to bring into your life. Note that the practices mentioned can be used in both underactive and overactive states.

Root Chakra (Grounding and Stability)

- **Imbalance**: Leaders who lack grounding may feel reactive, overwhelmed, or disconnected from the present moment. They may struggle with consistency and decision-making under pressure.
- **Impact**: Teams feel unsupported and uncertain, leading to reduced trust, lower morale, and instability within the organization.
- **Energy Practice**: Grounding breathwork, walking barefoot outside, or using visualization techniques that connect you to the earth.
- **Leadership Benefit**: Increases presence, reduces stress, and enhances decision-making under pressure.
- **Simple Ritual Example**:

  - Before a big meeting, take 60 seconds to ground yourself. Inhale deeply, visualize roots extending from your feet into the earth, and exhale any tension. Focus on longer-duration exhale—this activates the parasympathetic nervous system, helping you relax, dilate blood vessels, and reduce stress more effectively than simply slowing your breath. The ancient Yoga Sutras recommend an inhale-to-exhale ratio of 1:2 (e.g., inhale for four counts, exhale for eight), emphasizing smooth, silent, and rhythmic breathing.[1]
  - **Walking Meditation for Clarity**: Zohra learned from monks during time spent with them, who dedicate 10–15 minutes daily to a silent walk in nature. Sync your breath with your steps and focus on the present moment, releasing mental chatter. As you walk, ask: *What message is life trying to communicate to me today?* Stay open to any thoughts or insights that arise, reconnecting with nature's rhythm to promote clarity and intuitive insight.

Sacral Chakra (Creativity and Emotional Flow)

- **Imbalance**: Suppressed creativity, emotional volatility, or an inability to adapt to change can lead to either rigid leadership or emotional unpredictability.
- **Impact**: Teams experience tension, lack of collaboration, and diminished innovation, leading to stagnant growth and creative blocks.

- **Energy Practice:** Creative visualization, water-based relaxation exercises, or movement practices like dance or yoga.
- **Leadership Benefit:** Enhances EI, adaptability, and creative problem-solving.
- **Simple Ritual Example:** Start your day with a five-minute freewriting session or a brainstorming exercise to clear mental clutter and open the flow of creative thinking. This practice helps bridge the gap between subconscious insights and conscious thought, setting the tone for clarity and productivity throughout the day. To enhance this experience, incorporate sound frequencies that align with specific brainwave states. Using these sound frequencies, leaders can intentionally shift their brain state to align with their desired energy for the day—whether it's fostering creativity, deepening intuition, or enhancing structured decision-making.
- **Alpha Waves (8–14 Hz)—Relaxed Focus and Creativity**

  - **Solfeggio Frequency: 432 Hz**—Known as the "Natural Frequency of the Universe," this tone promotes clarity, relaxation, and creative inspiration.
  - **Example:** Listen to soft instrumental music tuned to 432 Hz while journaling or mapping out ideas to enhance problem-solving and lateral thinking.
- **Theta Waves (4–8 Hz)—Deep Reflection and Intuition**

  - **Solfeggio Frequency: 528 Hz**—Often called the "Miracle Tone," this frequency is believed to promote transformation, clarity, and heightened awareness.
  - **Example:** Use 528 Hz binaural beats during morning visualization exercises or meditative reflection to set clear leadership intentions for the day.
- **Beta Waves (14–30 Hz)—Active Thinking and Productivity**

  - **Solfeggio Frequency: 741 Hz**—Associated with clarity and expression, this frequency helps with problem-solving and structured thinking.
  - **Example:** Play 741 Hz frequencies in the background while reviewing strategic plans or preparing for important meetings to enhance cognitive processing.[2]

Solar Plexus Chakra (Confidence and Purpose)

- **Imbalance:** Leaders may struggle with either arrogance—alienating their teams—or fear of failure, leading to hesitation and indecision.
- **Impact:** Teams feel micromanaged, disempowered, or uncertain about the leader's ability to guide them effectively.

- **Energy Practice**: Power postures, personal affirmations, and visualization exercises that reinforce confidence.
- **Leadership Benefit**: Strengthens self-assurance, assertiveness, and decision-making clarity.
- **Simple Ritual Example**: Before a major presentation, take a power stance, close your eyes, and repeat the affirmation: *I lead with confidence and purpose.* With the power pose, incorporate the powerful breathwork exercise called the 4–7–8 breathing, developed by Dr. Andrew Weil, based on ancient pranayama practices. In order to receive the benefits of calming the nervous system, reducing stress, or improving sleep, you inhale through your nose for four seconds, hold your breath for seven seconds, and exhale slowly and fully through your mouth for eight seconds.[3] Repeating this a handful of times enhances emotional regulation, while building long-term resilience for the modern leader.

Heart Chakra (Compassion and Connection)

- **Imbalance**: Leaders may overextend themselves emotionally, leading to burnout, or appear detached, creating a sense of disconnection.
- **Impact**: Teams feel unsupported, undervalued, or emotionally burdened, affecting engagement and retention.
- **Energy Practice**: Gratitude journaling, heart-focused breathing, and intentional acts of kindness.
- **Leadership Benefit**: Builds trust, fosters team cohesion, and cultivates psychological safety.
- **Simple Ritual Example**: End each day by acknowledging one meaningful contribution from a team member and letting go of one thing that doesn't serve you or your team. A consistent practice of letting go will open more space for you to receive greater insights, invitations, and intuition. It is also far easier than you think. Here is how you can practice it:

    - Identify an unresolved tension—a past disagreement, resentment, or lingering frustration. It can be worrying about your company's financial welfare, fear of whether a deal will go through, sadness about losing a client to another firm, or doubt that you will hit your budget targets for the year. Regardless of what it is, when you consciously create the space to let go of the things no longer serving you, you make room for greater energetic abundance to flow into your life.
    - Write it down, followed by: *I forgive and release this for my peace and growth.*
    - Visualize letting go of the weight, seeing it dissolve like mist.

- In addition, you can also try the compassion pause ritual. This strengthens trust and collaboration and reduces miscommunication and reactive responses. Here is how you can practice it.
  - Before responding to a colleague or team member, pause for two to three seconds.
  - Follow the 70/30 Rule—listen for 70% of the time, and speak for 30%.
  - After someone speaks, pause for three to five seconds before responding to ensure full absorption of their message.
  - Ask yourself: *Am I listening to understand or to respond?*
  - Maintain eye contact and observe body language to fully absorb their message.
  - Repeat back or summarize their point to ensure clarity before responding.
  - When responding, summarize what you heard before offering your own perspective.

Throat Chakra (Communication and Authenticity)

- **Imbalance**: Leaders may either dominate conversations—over-explaining and leaving little space for others—or struggle with self-expression, failing to articulate vision and direction.
- **Impact**: Teams experience misalignment, confusion, and a lack of psychological safety, which stifles innovation and trust.
- **Energy Practice**: Mindful pauses before speaking, Throat Chakra chanting, and practicing active listening.
- **Leadership Benefit**: Improves clarity, strengthens team alignment, and enhances authentic communication.
- **Simple Ritual Example**: Before entering important conversations, presentations, or decision-making moments, pause for a truth check-in by asking: *Is what I am about to say truthful, necessary, and kind?* Pair this with Box Breathing—a technique used by Navy SEALs, elite athletes, and meditators to enhance focus, composure, and emotional regulation before high-stakes situations. It works to regulate the nervous system, preventing stress-based reactivity in conversations. It also enhances verbal clarity and emotional balance, ensuring that communication is deliberate and impactful. Lastly, it creates a moment of pause, allowing space for conscious speech rather than impulsive reaction.[4]
  - Here is how to practice Box Breathing
  - Inhale deeply through the nose for four seconds.

- Hold your breath for four seconds.
- Exhale slowly through the mouth for four seconds.
- Hold the breath again for four seconds.
- Repeat this cycle four to five times or until a sense of calm focus emerges.

- Alternatively, you can try the Throat Chakra expansion techniques for power and presence in speech, authentic expression journaling for communication clarity, and a listening reset practice. These practices enhance presence and authority in communication while reducing rushed speech and verbal clutter, ensuring that your words carry impact.

  - **Practice Power and Presence:**
    - Before speaking in a meeting or presentation, visualize your words carrying clarity and strength.
    - Drop your voice slightly into a grounded, lower register for confidence.
    - Speak deliberately and with intention, avoiding filler words.
    - Use pauses effectively to let messages resonate.

  - **Practice Authentic Expression Journaling:**
    - At the start or end of the day, free-write for five to ten minutes on the following prompts using the Solfeggio frequencies mentioned in the Sacral Chakra section above. Do not edit—just write freely to clear mental noise and align thoughts with intentional speech. You will be surprised at what you write when you permit yourself to be free. This freedom is where you get closer to the parts of you that have been waiting to be seen and heard.
      - *What is one message I need to communicate with clarity today?*
      - *Where am I holding back from expressing my truth?*
      - *How can I ensure my words align with my leadership values?*

Third Eye Chakra (Intuition and Vision)

- **Imbalance:** Leaders may become fixated on narrow perspectives or get lost in overanalyzing, delaying action and preventing forward momentum.
- **Impact:** Teams miss opportunities for innovation and struggle to adapt to changing circumstances.
- **Energy Practice:** Reflective journaling, meditation, and strategic visualization exercises.

- **Leadership Benefit**: Enhances foresight, improves problem-solving, and deepens intuitive decision-making.
- **Simple Ritual Example**: Start each week by visualizing the best outcomes for your key projects. Visualization aligns intention with action, and when combined with meditation, it boosts focus, decision-making, and confidence. Research by Dr. Amishi Jha shows that just 12 minutes of daily meditation improves attention, memory, and cognitive resilience, even in high-stress professions.[5]

How to Practice Visualization Meditation:

1 **Find a Comfortable Seat**: Sit upright with a straight spine.
2 **Align Your Posture**: Keep your chin parallel to the floor, neck and back aligned.
3 **Position Your Hands**: Rest them on your thighs or abdomen, palms up.
4 **Soften Your Eyes**: Close or half-close with a gentle downward gaze.
5 **Focus on the Third Eye**: Direct awareness to the space between your eyebrows.
6 **Breathe Deeply**: Inhale through your nose, expanding your belly.
7 **Release Tension**: Tense your body for six counts to release stress.
8 **Exhale and Let Go**: Forcefully exhale through the mouth, repeating three times.
9 **Return to Natural Breathing**: Observe your breath without controlling it.
10 **Visualize Success**: See yourself confidently leading, making strategic decisions, and overcoming challenges with ease.

Crown Chakra (Purpose and Universal Insight)

- **Imbalance**: Leaders may either become disconnected from practical execution—focusing too much on abstract vision—or feel uninspired, losing sight of their deeper mission.
- **Impact**: Teams feel disengaged, lacking a clear sense of purpose and alignment with organizational goals.
- **Energy Practice**: Meditation, intention setting, and periodic solitude for reflection.
- **Leadership Benefit**: Strengthens alignment with a greater purpose, preventing burnout and disconnection.
- **Simple Ritual Example**: Start each morning by setting an intention that aligns your daily actions with your long-term mission. This practice sharpens focus, willpower, and clarity, tapping into the Crown Chakra's energy of wisdom and purpose. While deep meditative states like *samadhi* require years of practice, leaders can access moments of expanded awareness through simple techniques.

How to Practice:

1 **Find a Quiet Space:** Sit in a calm, distraction-free area, ideally with natural light.

2 **Adopt a Comfortable Posture:** Sit cross-legged or in a chair with a straight spine, palms facing upward.

3 **Breathe Deeply:** Inhale through your nose, exhale through your mouth, repeating three times to clear mental clutter.

4 **Activate the Crown Chakra:** Visualize a violet or white light at the top of your head, expanding with each breath.

5 **Set Your Intention:** Ask, *How can I lead with wisdom and purpose today?* Allow an answer to arise naturally.

6 **Enter Stillness:** Focus on the space between thoughts, returning to stillness when distractions arise.

7 **Visualize Your Highest Self:** See yourself leading with intuition, grace, and alignment to your mission.

8 **Seal with Gratitude:** End by acknowledging something you're grateful for—a lesson, challenge, or opportunity.

This simple ritual fosters clarity, purpose, and intentional leadership throughout your day.

Beyond meditation, there are other powerful ways, that is, mind mapping, sacred reading, to activate the Crown Chakra and integrate higher awareness into leadership. Mind mapping activates both hemispheres of the brain, unlocking creativity and holistic problem-solving that aligns with long-term vision. Sacred reading helps engage with profound wisdom regularly and expands awareness, deepens intuition, and aligns daily decisions with higher purpose. Here is how to practice:

- **Mind-Mapping:**

  - Write a central theme or leadership challenge in the middle of a blank page.
  - Without overthinking, branch out ideas, solutions, and insights, allowing creativity to flow.
  - Observe emerging patterns—these spontaneous connections often reveal higher-order wisdom that the conscious mind might overlook.

- **Sacred Reading and Contemplation**

  - Choose a passage from a wisdom text (Tao Te Ching, Bhagavad Gita, Rumi, or even leadership philosophy).
  - Read one passage mindfully and reflect: How does this apply to my leadership today?
  - Journal a brief response, allowing insights to emerge.

Note: These breathing and mindfulness techniques are not a substitute for medical advice. Consult a healthcare professional if you have conditions like high blood pressure, respiratory issues, heart disease, pregnancy, or other concerns. Always practice safely and avoid hazardous environments, such as driving or water-related activities.

Whether through meditation, creative visualization, nature immersion, or deep contemplation, the key to sustaining high-impact leadership lies in developing a daily practice of expansion—one that elevates leadership beyond strategy into a sacred responsibility that serves the greater whole. True leadership is not just about execution; it's about energy. Leaders who manage their energy effectively create workplaces where focus, trust, and engagement thrive. Mastering energy management isn't about adding more to your plate—it's about shifting how you show up. Small, intentional micro-adjustments practiced consistently, create lasting transformation.

Six Second Memory: The Art of Letting Go

One of the most critical concepts in both leadership resilience and spiritual growth is the art of letting go. The stories we accumulate over time shape our self-perception and leadership narratives. However, if we cling too tightly to past experiences—whether failures or successes—we risk letting them define our present and dictate our future.

In American football, the average play lasts six seconds. If a player misses a tackle, drops a pass, or fumbles the ball, dwelling on that moment can disrupt their ability to perform in the next play or the rest of the game. If they ruminate on failure—beating themselves up for lost opportunities—their lack of self-compassion and mental distraction can spiral into weaker performance over time.

This is where the six-second memory principle becomes a powerful leadership tool. For six seconds, the player is fully engrossed in the moment, responding with clarity and agility. After those six seconds, they extract the lesson from the play, release the attachment, and move forward. This practice trains football players to let go of past mistakes, unmet expectations, or external pressures and instead show up fully in the present (lessons of the Crown Chakra).

For the Chakra Leader, the equivalent of the six-second memory is resilience. If a decision goes poorly, own it, extract the lesson, and devise a new path forward. There is no value in dwelling on what could have been. Instead, use every challenge as an opportunity to refine your wisdom, sharpen your intuition, and emerge stronger. Great leaders do not avoid failure—they master how to move through it.

This ability to pivot, adapt, and reset is what separates leaders who thrive from those who stagnate. Energy management, self-mastery, and resilience are therefore the foundations of sustainable leadership. When you regulate your energy, align with your purpose, and cultivate inner balance, you create a leadership legacy that is not only impactful but also transformational.

References

1. Van Diest, I., Verstappen, K., Aubert, A. E., Widjaja, D., Vansteenwegen, D., & Vlemincx, E. (2014). Inhalation/exhalation ratio modulates the effect of slow breathing on heart rate variability and relaxation. *Applied Psychophysiology and Biofeedback, 39*(3), 171–180. https://doi.org/10.1007/s10484-014-9253-x
2. Yang, X., Nah, F., & Lin, F. (2023). A review on the effects of chanting and Solfeggio frequencies on well-being. In *Lecture notes in computer science* (Vol. 14082, pp. 628–639). Springer. https://doi.org/10.1007/978-3-031-48041-6_42
3. Weil, A. (n.d.). 4-7-8 breathing exercise. *DrWeil.com*. Retrieved from https://www.drweil.com/health-wellness/body-mind-spirit/stress-anxiety/
4. Balban, M. Y., Neri, E., Kogon, M. M., Weed, L., Nouriani, B., Jo, B., Holl, G., Zeitzer, J. M., Spiegel, D., & Huberman, A. D. (2023). Brief structured respiration practices enhance mood and reduce physiological arousal. *Cell Reports. Medicine, 4*(1), 100895. https://doi.org/10.1016/j.xcrm.2022.100895
5. Jha, A. P. (2021). *Peak mind: Find your focus, own your attention, invest 12 minutes a day*. HarperOne.

Chapter 12

Chakras for Transforming Teams and Organizations

Source: iStock.com/JulyProkopiv

DOI: 10.4324/9781003635918-13

The Bridge: Leadership and Team Energy Management

There's a common saying, "If you want to go fast, go alone; but if you want to go far, go together." Leadership is not a solo endeavor—it is a shared journey, deeply intertwined with the energy of those around us. Much like the human body functions through interconnected systems, a thriving workplace operates as a unified organism. Just as different organs serve specific functions, every person brings unique gifts, skills, and insights that play a vital role in contributing to collective success.

Imagine a rural or tribal village where survival and progress depend on interdependence. There are farmers, healers, hunters, builders, and leaders—all playing a crucial role in sustaining the community. No single person can do it all, nor are they meant to. Modern organizations are no different. The most effective teams mirror this ancient model, where each member's strengths and contributions fuel a well-balanced, thriving system.

One of our most basic energetic needs, as seen in the Root Chakra, is a deep sense of tribal and communal belonging. When a leader embodies this principle, they act as a beacon of coherence, naturally entraining the energy of those around them. This is not an abstract concept—it is the fundamental law of resonance at work. Just as a finely tuned instrument can make others vibrate in tandem, a balanced leader fosters alignment within their team, elevating collective morale and performance.

This principle applies beyond leadership—it extends into every aspect of life. Consider the pursuit of financial abundance. True prosperity does not come from merely wishing for wealth; rather, it begins with an internal shift in perspective. If you believe in lack, your actions unconsciously reflect scarcity. However, when you recognize that abundance is ever-flowing—just as money is printed daily—your mindset and actions align with that reality, and external circumstances adjust accordingly. Your external reality is always a reflection of your inner state.

Likewise, a Chakra Leader influences reality by embodying clarity, empowerment, and alignment. Leadership is not just about execution; it is about energetic responsibility—what you cultivate internally is reflected in the spaces you lead. When a leader embodies balance, clarity, and authenticity, the team naturally follows suit. Once these energetic principles are fully integrated on a personal level, the next step is to extend them into team practices—ensuring that the collective thrives, not just the individual. This is where emotional intelligence, servant leadership, and transformational leadership intersect with the chakra system, offering a structured yet fluid framework for creating a high-performing, holistic workplace. Interestingly, the most profound leadership shifts do not come from complex strategies—they arise from the simplest, yet most overlooked, principles.

At the heart of a truly cohesive team lies gratitude and love. The most energetically attuned leaders practice gratitude for every experience, not just the favorable ones. They embrace challenges, setbacks, and difficult clients as essential growth opportunities that refine leadership mastery. Similarly, leading from love instead of fear creates a profound energetic shift. A simple, yet powerful, self-reflective question can instantly recalibrate decision-making: "Am I making this choice from fear or love?" When energy practices become woven into the fabric of leadership, they elevate an organization's culture beyond conventional approaches.

Integrating Chakras into Team Dynamics

Leadership today is no longer solely about individual performance—it is about how teams collectively cultivate energy, connection, and purpose. A truly thriving organization is one that aligns not just minds, but hearts and spirits, integrating both modern leadership science and ancient energetic wisdom into team-building, strategy, and culture.

The timeless *Golden Rule*—"Treat others as you wish to be treated"— carries a profound meaning when viewed through a spiritually symbolic lens. We are all created from the same elements, the same stardust, and the same molecules. Beneath the surface, we share the same fundamental fears, aspirations, and longings for connection. Regardless of race, gender, or socioeconomic background, at our core, we are human. On the deepest spiritual level, there is a singularity of source consciousness that fractals infinitely into diverse physical manifestations. While the person across from you may seem completely different, they are simply another expression of the same universal light—another reflection of the same consciousness. How you treat others is ultimately how you treat yourself, for in the grand mirror of existence, all actions, words, and energies return to their source.

In the following section, we introduce seven team practices, each tied to a chakra and a key stage of the team life cycle. These exercises ensure that leaders cultivate a holistic, energetically aligned, and high-performing workplace—ensuring that team dynamics remain balanced, resilient, and deeply connected.

Root Chakra: Grounding New Hires with Intentional Onboarding Rituals

Stage: Onboarding and Team Formation: Creates trust, strengthens psychological safety, and builds deep organizational alignment.

- **Purpose:** The Root Chakra governs stability, belonging, and trust, making it the foundation for onboarding and team cohesion. A strong start ensures long-term retention, psychological safety, and organizational alignment.
- **Technique:** Welcome and Grounding Ritual

  - Begin onboarding with a grounding practice that connects new employees to the company's mission, vision, and long-term purpose.
  - Conduct a team story-sharing session, where senior members share the organization's journey and their personal "why."
  - Pair new hires with mentors or energy guides—longstanding team members who can serve as trusted allies in their transition.
  - Close with a ritual circle, where each team member shares their reason for being part of the organization, reinforcing a sense of belonging.

Sacral Chakra: The Cacao Ceremony— Fostering Emotional Connection & Creative Flow

Stage: Team Bonding and Emotional Alignment: Enhances EI, deepens trust, and creates a space for intuitive problem-solving and creative breakthroughs.

- **Purpose:** The Sacral Chakra is the center of EI, creativity, and authentic expression. Teams that cultivate openness and trust collaborate more deeply and innovate more freely.
- **Technique:** The Cacao Ceremony

  - Why cacao? Cacao has been used in indigenous ceremonies for centuries as a heart-opening and connective ritual, enhancing creativity and deepening relationships. Science has also shown that raw powdered cacao has nearly 40x the antioxidant properties of blueberries as measured on the ORAC (Oxygen Radical Absorbance Capacity) scale.
  - Before a strategic retreat, team offsite, or major project kickoff, gather the team for a sacred cacao ceremony.

A cacao ceremony fosters open-hearted communication, team connection, and intentional focus on shared goals. Cacao (*Theobroma Cacao*, meaning *Food of the Gods*) has been used in indigenous Central and South American rituals for centuries, believed to promote spiritual connection and emotional well-being. As a heart-opener, cacao influences neurotransmitters like dopamine and oxytocin, enhancing mood.

Note: Those with heart conditions, on antidepressants, pregnant, or breastfeeding should consult a doctor before participating.

Preparing Ceremonial Cacao:

- Use ceremonial-grade cacao with no added ingredients.
- For each serving: Mix 44g powdered cacao with 3–4 oz of water. Heat water just below simmer, add cacao, and stir until melted. Do not boil.
- Optional seasonings: Salt, cayenne (to activate), cinnamon, cardamom, nutmeg, rose powder, tahini, or vanilla.

Ceremony Steps:

1 Sit in a circle, each person holding their cacao.
2 Close eyes, tune into the cacao's energy.
3 Set a personal intention, whisper it into the cup, and take three mindful sips:

- **Sip 1**: Let go of the past.
- **Sip 2**: Embrace the present.
- **Sip 3**: Manifest the future.

Cacao effects emerge in 30–45 minutes. Engage in open discussions, creative brainstorming, or team-building activities like meditation, writing, or yoga to harness the energy.

Solar Plexus Chakra: Strength-Based Leadership and Personal Empowerment

Stage: Talent Development and Leadership Growth: Builds confidence, enhances self-motivation, and fosters a culture of accountability and leadership development.

- **Purpose**: The Solar Plexus Chakra governs confidence, motivation, and leadership identity. Leaders who understand their personal power uplift and empower their teams.
- **Technique: Personal Empowerment Mapping Session**

  - Replace traditional performance reviews with Solar Plexus Power Sessions to foster self-leadership and internal empowerment. These sessions help employees recognize their strengths, leadership potential, and personal mission, leading to greater engagement, confidence, and innovation.

How to Conduct the Session:

1 **Create a Relaxed Setting**: Meet in a comfortable space—whether in-person, outdoors, or virtually.
2 **Ground the Group**: Start with brief breathwork or a guided visualization to center focus.
3 **Set the Intention**: Example: *Today, we recognize our strengths, envision future success, and step into leadership power.*
4 **Future Visualization**: Have team members close their eyes and imagine themselves thriving in their roles two to three years from now—leading confidently, making decisions, and contributing meaningfully.
5 **Reflect and Write**: After visualizing, participants write down the qualities they embodied (e.g., resilience, creativity, and decisiveness).
6 **Strength Mapping**: Provide worksheets or whiteboards for mapping strengths and leadership growth areas. Use prompts like:

- *What are your top three strengths?*
- *What makes you feel powerful in leadership?*
- *What qualities do others recognize in you?*

7 **Create Leadership Affirmations**: Examples:

- *I am a confident leader who inspires through vision.*
- *I take bold action and trust in my success.*

8 **Speak Affirmations**: Pair participants to say affirmations aloud, reinforcing self-belief.
9 **Incorporate in Check-Ins**: Encourage leaders to revisit affirmations during regular feedback sessions.
10 **Group Reflection**: Share takeaways and commit to one action step to embody leadership power in the next month.

Optional: Have participants write a letter to their future selves detailing their vision and strengths, revisiting it in six months for reflection and growth.

Heart Chakra: Gratitude and Recognition Circles

Stage: Sustaining Engagement and Team Morale: Strengthens relationships, enhances emotional safety, and builds a culture of appreciation and fulfillment.

- **Purpose**: The Heart Chakra is the center of trust, appreciation, and emotional connection. It fuels recognition, collaboration, and long-term employee fulfillment.

- **Technique: Gratitude and Recognition Circles**
  - **Schedule Regularly:** Hold weekly, bi-weekly, or monthly sessions for 10–20 minutes during team meetings. Consistency is key.
  - **Create a Comfortable Space:** Gather in a distraction-free environment (in-person or virtual), using a circle setup to encourage openness.
  - **Ground the Group:** Start with a simple breath to focus everyone.
  - **Share Appreciation:** Each team member shares one thing they appreciate about a colleague—whether related to work, character, or small gestures.

    1 *Example*: "I appreciate [Name] for stepping up during tough discussions."

- **Reflect Silently:** Encourage reflection on:

  1 One thing they're grateful for at work.
  2 A teammate who made their job easier.
  3 A personal contribution they're proud of.

- **Enhance with Visuals:**

  1 Use a **Gratitude Board** or **Kudos Wall** for written notes of appreciation.
  2 Create a **Gratitude Jar** and read notes aloud monthly.
  3 For remote teams, use Slack channels or digital whiteboards for virtual recognition.

This simple, consistent ritual fosters connection, boosts morale, and strengthens team dynamics.

- Ongoing Practice.
- Encouraging Daily Micro-Gratitude Practices.
- Challenge employees to take 30 seconds at the end of each day to reflect on one meaningful moment from work.
- This could be a great conversation, a small win, or even a lesson learned.
- Over time, this simple habit shifts workplace culture toward positivity, appreciation, and emotional well-being.

Throat Chakra: Conscious Conversation and Business Manifestation Ceremony

Stage: Vision Alignment and Team Strategy: Aligns teams to a shared mission, deepens commitment, and fuels purpose-driven action.

- **Purpose:** The Throat Chakra governs communication, clarity, and expression—making it essential for visionary leadership and collective alignment.

- **Technique:** Business Manifestation Ceremony

    - Replace traditional strategic planning with a guided visualization to align team goals and vision.
      1 **Create a Comfortable Space:** Gather in a relaxed setting with enough room for everyone to sit or lie down.
      2 **Guided Breathwork:** Begin with breathwork to help each person connect to their vision for the business, team, or goals.
      3 **Sharing Circle:** After the session, have team members share their insights and work toward a unified vision.
      4 **Visualize Success:** As a group, visualize a future event where the shared goal is achieved. Set a future date for this vision.
      5 **Collective Meditation:** Close your eyes and imagine the journey toward that success, experiencing the growth and wisdom gained along the way.
      6 **Embed the Vision:** Feel the vision deeply, placing a hand over your heart. Silently affirm, *May this or something better happen.*
      7 **Release & Share:** Send these intentions outward with hands in a prayer position. Open your eyes and invite the team to share their experiences.

This ceremony helps embed a collective vision, fostering alignment, purpose, and team unity.

Third Eye Chakra: Vision Board Goal-Setting

Stage: Strategy Execution and Long-Term Growth: Strengthens intuitive decision-making, clarifies long-term priorities, and fosters collective ownership over success.

- **Purpose:** The Third Eye Chakra governs intuition, foresight, and visionary thinking, making it the key to long-term team strategy and innovation.

- **Technique:** Vision Board Strategy Sessions

    - **Create an Inspiring Space:** Gather in a comfortable setting like a conference room, retreat space, or outdoors.
    - **Mindful Start:** Begin with meditation or deep breathing to help the team connect with their aspirations.
    - **Set the Tone:** Share an opening statement. For example, *Today, we step into the future we wish to create.* Play calming background music to inspire creativity.

- **Personal Reflection:** Have team members journal on questions like:
  - *What is my vision for personal growth in the next one to five years?*
  - *How can our team evolve and make an impact?*
  - *What values or skills will I contribute to our collective vision?*
- **Create Vision Boards:** Provide creative materials (posters, magazines, and markers) for participants to visualize:
  - *Personal career goals.*
  - *Team mission.*
  - *Desired culture and energy.*
- **Share and Connect:** Each person presents their board, explaining the symbols and images. Look for shared themes and values.
- **Build a Team Vision:** Combine key elements from individual boards into a large team vision board. Display it prominently in the office or virtual workspace as a daily reminder of the team's purpose.
- **Commit and Reflect:** Have each team member write a personal commitment based on the session, e.g., *I commit to fostering open communication and trust.*
- **Follow-Up:** Schedule three- and six-month check-ins to revisit the vision board and assess progress toward goals.

This session aligns individual aspirations with team goals, fostering creativity, connection, and a shared vision for success.

Crown Chakra: Leadership Reflection and Collective Meditation

Stage: Sustaining Organizational Purpose and Legacy: Strengthens organizational culture, sustains purpose-driven leadership, and fosters a long-term commitment to shared vision.

- **Purpose:** The Crown Chakra governs higher purpose, unity, and spiritual alignment, ensuring that teams stay connected to a mission beyond daily operations.
- **Technique:** Leadership Meditation Ritual
  - **Create a Calm Space:** Use a quiet office, off-site retreat, or virtual setting with calming music.

- **Set the Purpose:** Explain the goal—This meditation helps us align our energy as leaders, focusing on the impact and legacy we create beyond business metrics.
- **Ground the Team:** Have participants sit comfortably, feet grounded, hands open, eyes closed.

- **Guided Breathwork:** Use Box Breathing (inhale, hold, exhale, and hold for four seconds each) for five cycles to relax and focus.
- **Visionary Meditation:**

  - *Imagine yourself five years from now in a workplace shaped by your leadership—filled with trust, creativity, and fulfillment. What do you feel, see, and experience?*
  - *See your leadership's ripple effect on your industry, community, and beyond. How have you contributed to something greater than business success?*

- **Gratitude Circle:** After meditation, share:

  - *One leadership quality you're grateful for in yourself.*
  - *One colleague or mentor you appreciate.*
  - *One recent moment that reminded you of your purpose.*

- **Write Key Insights:** Have participants note a leadership mantra or commitment for the next quarter.

  - *Examples: I commit to leading with patience, or I will prioritize well-being over burnout.*

- **Closing Reflection:** Guide a grounding breath and close with:

  - *As you exhale, send this clarity into your leadership journey ahead, knowing your impact has already begun.*

This ritual fosters clarity, gratitude, and purpose, strengthening leadership focus and team connection.

True leadership is about cultivating a cohesive energetic field where people feel empowered, engaged, and aligned with a shared purpose. The practices outlined in this chapter are more than just team-building exercises; they are tools that allow leaders to create workplaces rooted in trust, vision, EI, and holistic well-being. By integrating CL practices, teams no longer operate in silos but function as interconnected systems— where each individual contributes their unique strengths and higher potential to the collective mission.

However, transformation does not happen overnight. Just as individual energy work requires consistent self-awareness and recalibration, team energy management is an ongoing process. The most successful leaders recognize that culture is not something that is written on a wall or confined to a mission statement—it is something that is lived, breathed, and felt in every interaction.

For organizations that are ready to take this work deeper, we (Neal and Zohra) offer tailored workshops, training sessions, and executive coaching programs designed to help teams integrate these energy practices into their daily operations. Whether it's aligning leadership with a higher vision, fostering team synergy, or implementing conscious communication techniques, we work with companies to cultivate energetically balanced workplaces that drive innovation, resilience, and long-term impact. If your team or organization is interested in customized leadership training, corporate retreats, or immersive CL coaching, we invite you to reach out.

The journey to high-impact leadership starts with energy alignment—because when leaders are balanced, teams thrive and organizations flourish.

Conclusion

The Lifelong Journey of the
Chakra Leader

Source: iStock.com/Benjavisa

DOI: 10.4324/9781003635918-14

Lifelong Self-Reflection and Chakra Alignment

This chapter serves as a reminder that leadership is not a fixed state—it is an ongoing, ever-evolving journey of self-awareness, growth, and transformation. True leadership is not measured solely by external achievements but by the depth of inner work one is willing to undertake. The most exceptional leaders are not those who merely accumulate power or accolades but those who courageously confront their own shadows, continuously refine their energetic alignment, and cultivate a deep sense of purpose beyond personal success.

The phrase "doing the work" is often used in personal development and leadership circles, yet this work is not about pitch decks, legal documents, or client deliverables. The work is the inner journey—the process of healing, integrating, and aligning with the highest version of yourself. It is the ongoing commitment to self-inquiry, emotional regulation, and spiritual awareness that ultimately defines the Chakra Leader.

We also have realized through our own journeys that this work (including shadow work) is not easy, nor is it ever truly complete. There will always be new lessons to learn, new perspectives to embrace, and new areas for growth. Moreover, confronting our shadows requires courage—the willingness to acknowledge where we are out of alignment, to face the discomfort of unlearning conditioned habits, and to reframe ego-driven fears into opportunities for transformation. However, for those who commit to this inner work, the rewards are profound: greater resilience, deeper wisdom, and a more authentic, impactful leadership presence.

- Shadow work requires deep introspection—examining limiting beliefs, unconscious fears, and conditioned patterns that inhibit one's ability to lead with authenticity.
- Energy management is a lifelong practice, ensuring that leaders remain centered, purposeful, and emotionally balanced amidst challenges.
- Self-transcendence is the ultimate goal, where leadership moves beyond personal ambition into a space of service, guiding teams and organizations toward collective well-being and greater impact.

Through reflective journaling, meditation, breathwork, and chakra alignment practices, leaders develop a heightened awareness of their energy, allowing them to lead with intention rather than reaction. These are not one-time fixes or quick solutions. They are lifelong habits—tools for self-reflection, realignment, and sustained leadership balance. By leading with aligned energy and purpose, Chakra Leaders create ripple effects of trust, collaboration, and innovation that extend far beyond themselves.

However, those who ignore the deeper work often encounter challenges that limit their leadership potential:

- Unaddressed Shadow Aspects: Without engaging in shadow work, leaders may unknowingly perpetuate fear, overcontrol, avoidance, or emotional disconnection, harming team trust, morale, and performance. This leads to ongoing imbalances, as we spoke in depth within this book.
- Stagnation in Leadership Growth: Many leaders fail to prioritize continuous learning and personal evolution, leading to a lack of adaptability, creativity, and vision.
- Disconnection from Impact: Leaders who neglect self-awareness and energetic alignment underestimate how their presence, words, and leadership style influence those around them.
- Neglect of Sustained Alignment: Leadership can become reactive rather than intentional, with little attention given to maintaining internal balance and alignment, reducing long-term effectiveness and fulfillment.

You may have heard that *the present moment is a present.* Each moment is a brand-new gift. No one instance is the exact same as the last. Life feels stagnant only when you stop taking an interest in growth. The Chakra Leader knows that the journey of life is indeed a marathon. Through a clear intention and consistent effort, change occurs in a matter of just a few years or less. The greatest gift you can offer any other person, team, or organization is to work on yourself. When you bring your blind spots into focus through self-awareness, you are no longer acting out of unconscious patterns or habits.

For a leader of an organization to do the real inner work of healing, longstanding, unconscious, or limiting belief patterns is the greatest show of dedication to their team and corporate culture. The difficult parts of you that you don't accept may live in the shadow because you're afraid of what these traits mean about you. However, when you consciously create the space to utilize mindful practices in your personal growth and healing journey, you bring these shadows into the light. With compassion and understanding, you realize that these parts of you are not meant to feel shameful or guilty about, but have been there as a mechanism to get you to where you are today. They served a purpose in some place, at some time; otherwise, they would not have been there. When you are ready to let go of those patterns that no longer serve you and integrate those which do through the lens of your Higher Self, you are well on your way to remembering your wholeness.

Few are aware enough to realize where they are holding themselves back. Even fewer are willing to do the work of stepping into their darkness to bring it into the light. If we are to evolve as individuals, leaders, corporations of influence, and collective consciousness, the journey toward that change starts with you and starts within. Through your daily actions and choices, you can shine with a frequency of light and strength that sets you apart from the crowd of mundane leaders and dime-a-dozen executives. This is the work of the Chakra Leader.

Honor and utilize your strengths to lift up your weaknesses. You are meant to fall in love with the process, not just the outcome. The end result is the final 1% of the journey. The 99% it takes to get you there is where the growth, experience, learning, and wisdom come from—through all of its ups and downs. In the end, you will find yourself at a completely different level of self-mastery than you ever could have imagined.

The Future of Leadership: Integrating Consciousness and Well-Being

The modern corporate landscape is shifting. As organizations grapple with burnout, disengagement, and cultural transformation, leaders are being called to evolve beyond traditional leadership models.

Recent surveys have shown that the top two priorities for HR and corporate leadership are:

1 **Leadership and Manager Development**: Building emotionally intelligent, conscious leaders who foster well-being and innovation.
2 **Organizational Culture Transformation**: Shifting from outdated, transactional leadership to a more holistic, people-centered approach.[1]

Throughout this book, we discussed how true leadership transformation begins within. We dived into shadow work, EI, energy alignment, and the power of conscious leadership—not as abstract concepts but as essential tools for navigating the rapidly evolving world of business and human connection. We stand at a critical junction in history where leadership is no longer just about power, strategy, or results—it's about energy. Holistic human well-being is fueling the next leadership transformation; and the leaders of the future will be those who know how to work with energy—their own, their teams', and their organizations'.

This is why micropractices like breathwork, gratitude journaling, meditation, creative visualization, and reflective self-inquiry are no longer optional. They are the new bedrock of long-term sustainable leadership, ensuring that leaders operate from a place of balance rather than burnout, inspiration rather than exhaustion, and intention rather than reaction. These are not fringe wellness trends—they are the new frontier of leadership development.[2]

To understand the shift happening in leadership today, we must revisit a pivotal moment in psychological history. In 1943, Abraham Maslow introduced self-actualization as the pinnacle of human potential—the realization of one's fullest capabilities. Yet, nearly three decades later, he expanded this concept to include something even greater: self-transcendence.[3]

Self-transcendence moves beyond personal achievement and into a higher realm of meaning, service, and collective impact. This shift is at the very heart of CL—a leadership model that elevates individual growth into a force for greater transformation.

- The Servant Leader prioritizes the well-being of others, leading with empathy, humility, and integrity.
- The Bodhisattva Leader embodies wisdom and compassion, uplifting others while remaining deeply committed to personal evolution.
- The Chakra Leader recognizes that personal energy is the foundation of organizational energy—that a leader's inner alignment is directly reflected in the external culture they create.

In this new paradigm, leaders are the Chief Energy Officers. They set the energetic tone of their organization, creating workplaces where clarity, trust, and purpose thrive.

A New Paradigm Begins

YOU made it.

Reaching the end of this book is not just about turning the final page—it's a testament to the time, energy, and intention you have invested in your own growth as a leader. For that, we honor you.

This book was written with heart and soul, a culmination of the wisdom and insights we were fortunate enough to grasp through our own experiences. The journey has not always been easy. It requires deep introspection, a willingness to confront discomfort, and a commitment to evolving beyond past limitations. But as we've discovered firsthand, the juice is worth the squeeze.

Through these pages, we have not only explored the chakras as energetic centers but have also worked to normalize spirituality in the workplace. After all, when leaders speak of bringing their full selves to work, how can that be possible without acknowledging the soul, energy, and inner wisdom that make us whole? This book serves as a bridge—a way to bring ancient wisdom into modern business, creating workplaces where leaders operate from alignment, teams thrive, and collective transformation takes root.

We also explored the shadows that create imbalances in leadership—the unhealed fears, insecurities, and conditioned behaviors that continue to manifest in the workplace. It is crucial to recognize these patterns so that we can break the cycle. The trauma of toxic corporate cultures and outdated leadership models does not need to be inherited by future generations. As leaders, we have the power to rewrite the narrative and to cultivate organizations that foster trust and well-being instead of burnout and detachment. That is the power which lies with YOU.

Envisioning Your Chakra Leader

Take a moment. Close your eyes.

Imagine what it feels like to be a fully embodied Chakra Leader. Feel it as if it's happening now.

Ask yourself:

- How do I show up at work?
- What do I think about in my free time?
- What kind of words do I use? Are these different from the words I use now?
- How do I support and uplift my team and employees?
- What matters most to me?
- How does my energy feel now relative to how it used to feel?
- What kind of distractions have I removed from my life?
- In what ways am I more intentional about all of my work and goals?
- How do I communicate with others? What has changed in my communication style?
- How has being a Chakra Leader in the workplace affected the energy of others?
- How has being a Chakra Leader shifted my personal life?
- What kind of activities or practices do I utilize in my daily life? When and why?
- What shadows have I become aware of and integrated?
- What chakra do I feel most personally connected to?
- What have I let go of?
- Why do these changes matter to me?
- What is my biggest takeaway from becoming an embodied Chakra Leader?

As you breathe life into these questions from your place of wholeness, visualize the impact being a Chakra Leader will have on your family, friends, community, organization, and even the world. Imagine the transformation your own shift will create for all of those who interact with you or consume the good/service you provide. Imagine how the clients you serve greatly benefit, your employees blossom under your guidance, and your organization brings in record financial abundance. See yourself shift the energy of others simply by bringing your full and balanced presence everywhere you go. This change all happened because you chose to lead with alignment, purpose, and integrity.

How does that feel?

Channel this energy and feeling as you think about your ultimate desire in life from the standpoint of being a Chakra Leader. Take some time to write down all of what you hope to accomplish and be as a result of this. Once you feel complete with this brainstorming, distill your desire down into a one- to two-sentence outcome known as a My Ultimate Desire (MUD) Statement. Write it out in the format of "My ultimate desire as a result of being a Chakra Leader is..."

Utilizing the chakra system as a leadership model offers a revolutionary approach to creating balanced, holistic workplaces. This new paradigm is built upon the foundation of love, trust, and energetic alignment. Imagine if the currency of business was love, and the value of a leader was measured by their ability to uplift and inspire.

How would your actions shift if the amount of love you gave was directly proportional to the abundance you received?

The answer lies in conscious reciprocity—a cycle where leadership becomes an exchange of energy rather than a transaction of tasks. In this space, gratitude, service, and authentic connection fuel both personal and organizational success.

A holistic workplace begins with personal energy awareness and self-mastery. When leaders balance their Root Chakra for stability, their Sacral Chakra for creativity, their Solar Plexus Chakra for confidence, their Heart Chakra for compassion, their Throat Chakra for communication, their Third Eye Chakra for vision, and their Crown Chakra for purpose, they set the tone for an organization that flourishes at every level.

When Western leadership science merges with Eastern spiritual wisdom, we unlock a leadership model that is not just effective, but transformative. Like a lotus rising from the mud, the shadows and outdated systems that have long weighed down corporate culture give way to a new kind of leadership—one rooted in awareness, integrity, and wholeness.

The Work Never Stops—And That's the Gift

As you continue this journey, know that the work does not stop here. The practices, reflections, and frameworks in this book are not meant to be passively absorbed—they are meant to be lived, refined, and embodied.

The traditional corporate model is no longer enough. Organizations that cling to outdated structures will struggle to adapt in an era where conscious leadership is the future.

The question is not whether leadership will change. It already is.

The question is: will you be a part of that change?

The most powerful corporations in the world set the tone for society. They shape cultures, influence millions, and determine the values that permeate workplaces and industries. When conscious, CL becomes the foundation of business; it transforms not just organizations, but the collective consciousness of humanity itself.

This book is only the beginning.

The real work starts now—in your daily decisions, your leadership presence, and the way you cultivate your team's energy.

For those who are ready to deepen this transformation, we invite you to connect with us and pave the way forward. Whether through:

- Executive coaching tailored to your leadership journey.
- Team energy alignment workshops to elevate workplace culture.
- Corporate training programs that integrate CL into real-world business practices.
- Or a simple hello followed with you sharing how your journey has been after this book.

We are here to support, guide, and co-create this shift with you. The future of leadership is energy, and you—as a Chakra Leader—are the one shaping it.

References

1. Gartner. (2023, October 17). *Where HR will focus in 2024.* https://www.gartner.com/en/articles/where-hr-will-focus-in-2024
2. CNET. (2024, February 8). *Top wellness trends to watch in 2025.* CNET. https://www.cnet.com/health/fitness/top-wellness-trends-to-watch-in-2025/
3. Maslow, A. H. (1969). The farther reaches of human nature. *Journal of Transpersonal Psychology, 1*(1), 1–9.

Index

For Product Safety Concerns and Information please contact our EU
representative GPSR@taylorandfrancis.com
Taylor & Francis Verlag GmbH, Kaufingerstraße 24, 80331 München, Germany

www.ingramcontent.com/pod-product-compliance
Lightning Source LLC
Chambersburg PA
CBHW052006270326
41929CB00015B/2813

9 781041 062981